GREAT HIDEOUTS OF THE WEST

An Idea Book for Living Free

BY BILL KAYSING

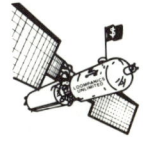

Loompanics Unlimited
Port Townsend, Washington 98368

ABOUT THE AUTHOR

Bill Kaysing has traveled extensively for more than 40 years in every Western state and is the author of several books on outasite living.

GREAT HIDEOUTS OF THE WEST
An Idea Book for Living Free
©1987 by Loompanics Unlimited
All Rights Reserved
Printed in the USA

Published by:
Loompanics Unlimited
PO Box 1197
Port Townsend, WA 98368

ISBN: 0-915179-62-8
Library of Congress Card Catalog Number 87-081103

TABLE OF CONTENTS

Preface 1
Short History of Hideouts 8
Parameters of a Hideout 13
Types of Hideouts 23
A Few Hideout Scenarios 38
Hideout Location Review 44
Photo Portfolio of Hideout Facilities 65
Floating Hideouts 105
Hot Spring Hideouts 132
The Ultimate Hideout 138
Self Defense for Your Hideout 142
Hideout Chow 146
A Miscellany 156
Summary and Conclusions 165
Bibliography 166

THE WEST

The map above presents the scope of this book in geographic form. We have also included a portion of lower British Columbia (shown later) for those who would like a Canadian caper. The eleven states shown represent millions of acres with much of it unpopulated or used by so few people on a regular basis that it is, for all purposes, vacant.

PREFACE

WHY HIDEOUTS?

In one sentence, you can't predict when you might need one.

Let me tell you about what happened to me in 1980.

I was in Las Vegas doing a series on tax rebellion for the *Las Vegas Sun*. A friend gave me a supply of the controversial solvent, DMSO (dimethyl sulfoxide) and asked if I would help distribute it. It seems that DMSO can be most helpful to people with aches and pains, twisted backs and sprains as well as the ubiquitous arthritis that plagues so many Americans. It was a revelation to see the material work so well and so fast with apparently no side effects. My enthusiasm grew and I became quite active, until the Las Vegas Police Department asked me politely but firmly to leave town.

No, there weren't any specific laws about DMSO, but when the LVPD asks you to do something, it's an offer you cannot refuse. Live there awhile, as I have, and you'll find this to be quite true.

So with a friend who had spent time as a marine in Vietnam, and a hooker who wanted to go straight, we loaded up the DMSO in my trusty pickup and headed for the cool breezes of Santa Barbara. Lots of old people there, I thought, who would welcome the soothing balm. There were, indeed, and our business boomed. At least until we got the word: the local DA was looking for us, armed with some charges of distributing pharmaceuticals without a license and practicing medicine sans an M.D.

We promptly moved ourselves and our stock of DMSO out of a friend's house and into a rather obscure little closet-like apartment on a quiet side street. There we pursued our efforts until one day my Vietnam friend said that he felt bad vibes, the same vibes that he had often felt in Nam before a disaster. So without further delay, we loaded up the DMSO and ourselves and left our cozy hideout just minutes before the DA's investigators arrived.

Now, I thought, what can we do? We wanted to hang around and give the community the benefit of DMSO, but on the other hand, it was obvious that we would be playing cat-and-mouse with the local Staats Polizei. What we really needed was a great hideout.

Author's rig: GMC pickup camper and Kenskill trailer down by the river and into the trees. Not new, not old, just unobtrusive and commonplace; exactly the type of movable hideout that most people wouldn't look at once, much less twice. Note bicycles on rear rack.

I drove up to Santa Cruz where I had a small travel trailer stored. When we arrived back in Santa Barbara we found a grove of old palm trees down by the railroad tracks and here we concealed the trusty old trailer. It became our home while we continued to make DMSO available to a lot of oldsters with the hurts.

We used bicycles to get around and at night were quiet as owls in our trackside hideout. Now that I think about it, the situation must have driven the DA a little wacko. Here, in his own hometown, were three people brashly breaking the law and he couldn't find them. And to add to his frustration, we often appeared on TV news after meeting the crew of the station at some isolated point!

Just to complete the story, the DA had to try us all *in absentia* and fine us $200,000.00 along with some other assorted punishments. But to this day, the three of us have avoided the long arm, thanks to a well-chosen hideout.

BUT IT COULDN'T HAPPEN TO YOU... OR COULD IT?

Sure, you probably won't be distributing DMSO or otherwise making the authorities unhappy. But what about some of the other reasons why a hideout might be just what you need?

Industrial and Natural Catastrophes

Bhopal, Three-Mile Island and Chernobyl along with dozens of other less lethal events have certainly pointed out that few places on earth are guaranteed safe. Even the little hamlet of St. George, Utah, got a severe dose of radiation after an atomic test at the Nevada test site. The people there are still suffering from its devastating effects. Furthermore, the deaths of John Wayne, Susan Hayward and Dick Powell, plus others, were attributed to being in St. George making a movie at the time of the test.

Earthquakes, hurricanes and other natural "Acts of God" are hard to predict and often impossible to avoid. But you can choose a hideout where these possibilities are minimized.

Counter-Culture Behavior

Some people believe in polygamy, nudity, use of herbal smokes and other activities which straight society deems harmful or unlawful. If you want to pursue your own private lifestyle free of hassles, then a hideout might be a perfect part- or full-time solution.

Collapse of Social Structures

The smart people of Beirut left what was once called the "Paris of the Middle East" before it became a chaotic shooting gallery. Wherever they went was their "hideout" and you must admit that almost *anyplace* would be heavenly compared to bombed-out Beirut. Today, there are many places on this planet (South Africa, Central America, any airport) where the chances of being perforated accidentally or intentionally are quite high.

Unjust Prosecution

Alan H. Nittler, M.D., was a creative and innovative physician who helped develop the science and practice of nutritional health known as orthomolecular therapy. He was fantastically successful...actually *too* successful. Thousands of patients were healed of their ills, often by nothing more than a simple change of diet and elimination of prescription drugs or over-the-counter nostrums. Eventually he wrote a bestseller, *A New Breed of Doctor*, which sold millions of copies in both hard cover and paperback.(I recommend you try to find it in your local library.)

All of this anti-allopathic (drug) activity attracted the attention of the power structure that dominates the medical scene in America. They proceeded to frame Alan, give him a mock trial and, after amputating his license to practice, destroyed him financially by bringing in the IRS. The stress of this bureaucratic assassination led to his death a few years ago.

With 20-20 hindsight it's clear that Dr. Nittler would have benefitted by having some sort of hideout where he could have pursued his work free of intervention by the AMA-drug-empire villains. It is noteworthy that many doctors have taken a cue from Nittler's case and now practice in a low-profile manner or have gone to foreign countries where medical liberty still exists.

A Simple Need for Peace and Quiet

Let's say that you are a poet, musician, composer, writer, sculptor or other creative person. Or perhaps you just enjoy silence and solitude. Obviously, a serene, sylvan hideout would be ideal for your psyche.

The Underground Economy

I'll call him Farmer Brown and delight in telling you that he reaped a lot of corn from a 600-acre hideout in a location that even the rack would not induce me to reveal. Brown is typical of millions of people who are enjoying the total fruits of their labors by operating from often plainly-visible "hideouts."

With taxes often taking half of a person's income, it's become almost mandatory to fight back and that's exactly what many tax avoiders are doing. And if it takes a hideout to do it, then obviously, that's what you will need.

Political Differences

The war between the haves and have-nots continues worldwide causing much socio-political strife. Imprisonment, torture and death are common in such totalitarian states as Chile, Argentina, parts of South Africa and Central America. In these regions, a hideout is absolutely essential.

As Big Brother becomes bigger and more pervasive in this, the largest of banana republics, hideouts may become the best sellers in real estate by the end of the 20th century. As you'll learn, later on in this book, there are quite a number of property firms touting far-off land bargains.

Communal Farms

Back-to-the-land Utopias are still prospering in many parts of the U.S. Although they do not qualify as hidden hideouts, they are usually located in remote areas to minimize bureaucratic interference.

Experimenters

I know a man who is working on a practical solution to the oil problem. He separates water into its components, oxygen and hydrogen, and uses the former to burn the latter in a specially modified internal combustion engine. Past efforts to perfect this system and thus free the world from petroleum domination have apparently been suppressed. My friend is taking precautions by doing all his development work in a most unique and clever hideout where I predict the bad guys will never find him.

Recovery from Ailments

Several years ago I was exploring the Panamint Valley on my motorcycle when I discovered an inhabited ghost town. Here were several people in their sixties and seventies enjoying good health after having been told they were terminal by urban physicians. It seems that pure air and good water plus a simple diet restored their health. And being in a remote, hideout-like location was undoubtedly a contributing plus factor.

Personally, I can't think of a better solution for the many physical, mental and spiritual ills that result from living in our current "air-conditioned nightmare" than escape to the peace and serenity of a remote hideout location. Quite recently I was able to compare downtown Seattle with the delights of Orcas Island in the San Juan Islands and I'll give you just one guess which locale won first prize.

In summary, there are virtually unlimited reasons why one should consider a hideout or, at the very least, learn about them, so that when the need arises, the expertise will be there. And that is exactly why this book was written.

A SHORT HISTORY OF HIDEOUTS

The campfire sent flashes of flickering light into the dark recesses of the cave. Gathered behind it and protected by its animal-repelling heat, the small group of cave-dwellers huddled close. Another long night of sheer survival was about to begin.

There's no question that hideouts have a long history. All over the world one can find rocky caves with the tell-tale coating of heavy smoke residues on the ceiling. Occasionally, primitive paintings tell us of the hopes, fears and dreams of our tough and persevering ancestors.

Hideouts have never lost their popularity and figure prominently down through history. In his recent book, *In Search of the Trojan War*, Mike Woods recounts the signs which indicate a systems collapse:

(1) The central political organization breaks up.

(2) The traditional ruling class disintegrates.

(3) The centralized economy collapses.

(4) There is widespread abandonment of settlements and ensuing depopulation. Towns and cities are left to be taken over by lower classes; there is often flight to the hills, *to isolated defensible spots*. (Our emphasis)

I was born in 1922; consequently, I have been a witness to the modern counterpart of the era that Woods describes (12th-century-B.C. Troy). In the early 30's, homeless men roamed along the railroad tracks of the small town in which I lived (South Pasadena, California). When they could, they built pitiful shacks from scrap wood and discarded signs.

Here they gathered about small fires, cooking what food they had been able to to scrounge from an already-poor neighborhood. One of my earliest recollections is being asked to "Run home, kid, and ask your mother if she'll let you give us a couple of spuds."

Often driven from their huts, the jobless men gathered in hobo jungles along creek beds, sheltered by willows and cottonwoods, and there built hideouts of a more or less permanent kind. Unfortunately, even in the relatively affluent region in which I now live (Santa Cruz, California) one can easily find contemporary hideouts in the dense redwood forests and these too are inhabited by the poor and homeless.

As the French say, the more things change, the more they stay the same.

In his classic work, *The Outline of History*, H.G. Wells gives a graphic description of conditions that precede the need for a place to be safe:

"Western Europe in the 8th century AD was a shattered civilization without law, without administration, with roads destroyed and education disorganized. It was a time of confusion, of brigandage, of crimes unpunished and universal insecurity. No man was safe."

Making another quantum leap in time, we find this passage in the same *Outline*:

"The tanks and screaming dive bombers drove packs of terrified civilians before them; the Allied forces, trying to march to aid the Belgians found themselves entangled in a mass of panic-struck refugees stampeding to the west. To add to the terror, the defenseless city of Rotterdam was raided by the Luftwaffe...."

The date? May, 1940.

Moving even closer to the present, we find the following in the June 2, 1986 issue of *Newsweek*:

The fire smoldered for four days, sending a mushroom cloud of smoke over the sprawling shantytown near Cape Town. When it was over, more than 3,000 of the tiny houses in Crossroads had burned to the ground and over a quarter of its population of 200,000 was left homeless. Thousands of displaced blacks sat on the roadsides, shivering in the winter cold, surrounded by salvaged scraps of bedding, clothing and kitchen utensils. There was no clue to where they would go — only that they could soon get caught again in the cross fire between the fathers and the comrades.

It is apparent that the fabric of our social structure is a delicate one. Unrest, war, natural disasters and other catastrophes can rip apart the seemingly secure safety net overnight. It's understandable why hideouts have been and still are a practical means of keeping one's body, mind and spirit neatly associated. Let's take a look at the evolution of the modern hideout.

FROM CAVES TO CAMPERS

As mentioned, caves were among the first hideouts of man. In time, these evolved into man-made caves; the stone structures that provided shelter both hidden and in view. However, as political or religious views became unpopular, many people reverted to cave life (the Essenes in their Dead Sea caves are a good example).

It is reasonably certain that many foresighted Romans fled to their prepared hideouts in southern and central Europe before and during the fall of the Roman Empire. During a recent tour of Italy and Austria, it was evident that such a transit could have been made. Once in the forested redoubts of Austria, relative safety would have been assured.

As the Dark Ages descended, a new type of hideout emerged, the strongly built, well-defended compound which later became the feudal castle of Arthurian legend. With moats, drawbridges, watchtowers and plenty of long-range arrows, the people who lived in these sophisticated and intelligently administrated enclaves were at least assured of reasonable safety.

In the Orient, giant counterparts of feudal architecture climaxed in the building of the Great Wall. This remarkable feat sought to make a hideout of millions of hectares of land and for a time was successful.

Although the Renaissance brought a modicum of order and stability plus new advances in the arts and sciences, life was still a tenuous matter in many parts of the world. Fighting went on almost continually somewhere or other on the troubled planet, from the War of the Roses to native rebellions, from Napoleonic Wars to the Blue and the Grey on our own soil. The other Horsemen of the Apocalypse were busy spreading doom in various areas with the result that retreats and hideouts gained in number and sophistication over the centuries.

What is a vacation home but a hideout from the stress of corporate life? What is a camper if not an updated gypsy wagon, quick and ready to move to safer spots on command?

Although the Industrial Revolution and the New Technology have wrought great changes for the world, it is still one that advisedly requires some thoughts about alternative locations, and that is what the hideout is all about.

Arrest and Search Warrants Prepared for Use in Connection with the Custodial Detention Program

Master Warrant of Arrest

WARRANT

To the Director of the Federal Bureau of Investigation:
 In pursuance of authority delegated to the Attorney General of the United States by Proclamation of the President of the United States, dated _____, 19___, I hereby authorize and direct you and your duly authorized agents to arrest or to cause the arrest of the persons whose names are set forth on the attached list and whom I deem dangerous to the public peace and safety of the United States.
 These persons are to be detained and confined until further order.
 I further authorize and direct you and your duly authorized agents, upon or subsequent to the arrest of any person set forth on the attached list and without regard to the place where such arrest may be made, to search any and all premises owned, occupied or controlled by such person, as well as any and all premises where such person is, or during the preceding twelve months period has been, employed or engaged in any regular activity, wherein it is believed that there may be found contraband, prohibited articles, or other materials in violations of the Proclamation of the President of the United States, dated _____, 19___, and as set forth in the Regulations issued pursuant thereto, and to seize and hold any such articles which you may find and make return thereof to the Attorney General.
 I further authorize and direct that this warrant may be executed at any hour of the day or night.
 By order of the President:

_____
Attorney General

Master Search Warrant

WARRANT   Dated: _____

To the Director of the Federal Bureau of Investigation:
 In pursuance of authority delegated to the Attorney General of the United States, by Proclamation of the President of the United States, dated _____, 19___, I hereby authorize and direct you and your duly authorized agents to make complete search of certain premises located and described on the attached list wherein it is believed that there may be found contraband, prohibited articles, or other materials in violation of the Proclamation of the President of the United States, dated _____, 19___, and as set forth in the Regulations issued pursuant therto, namely, firearms, weapons or implements of war or component parts thereof, ammunition, bombs, explosives or material used in the manufacture of explosives, short-wave radio receiving sets, transmitting sets, signal devices, codes or ciphers, cameras, means for promoting biological warfare, radioactive materials, atomic devices, or component parts thereof, propaganda material of the enemy or insurgents, propaganda material which fosters, encourages or promotes the policies, programs or objectives of the enemy or insurgents, printing presses, mimeograph machines, or other reproducing media on which such propaganda aforementioned has been or is being prepared, records, including membership and financial records of organizations or groups that have been declared subversive or may hereafter be declared subversive by the Attorney General, cash funds either in currency or coin, promissory notes or checks, securities of any nature, papers, documents, writings, code books, signal books, sketches, photographs, photograph negatives, blue prints, plans, maps, models, instruments, appliances, graphic representations, papers, documents, or books on which there may be invisible writing relating to or concerning any military, naval, or air, post, camp, station or installation or equipment or of any arms, ammunition, implements of war, devices or things used or intended to be used in the combat equipment of the land, naval or air forces of the United States, or of any military, naval, or air, post, camp, station or installation, and any and all files, dossiers, records, documents or papers of any kind which relate in any way to the identity, activities or operations of any person who is or may be engaged in espionage or sabotage against the interests of the United States.
 I further authorize and direct you to seize and hold any such articles which you may find and make return thereof to the Attorney General.
 I further authorize and direct that this warrant may be executed at any hour of the day or night.
 By order of the President:

_____
Attorney General

Dated: _____

These warrants exist and are ready for Big Brother's use when the occasion arises. So if you have ever had doubts about whether a hideout would be a worthwhile investment, these two master warrants should dispel them.

12

PARAMETERS OF A HIDEOUT

The term "parameter" was a popular term in aerospace in the '50's. Among a number of meanings it implied a list of essentials for a particular project or process. So let's review the absolute basics for safe and comfortable living in your hideout, whether it's a soundproof lab in Las Vegas or a gold dredge in the Mother Lode.

FOOD, AIR, WATER

SHELTER (Can be optional in some areas.)

CLOTHING (Might be optional in warm climates.)

Short list, isn't it? And it should be, considering that millions of mammals do just fine with the first line alone! However, as humans, we enjoy something more than just bread alone. Thus, to our absolute basic list we might add (and remember these are totally optional since we *can* live without them):

BATHING FACILITIES (Hot springs are a great alternative.)

SANITATION FACILITIES (What do bears do in the woods?)

COMFORTABLE BED (Ever try balsam boughs?)

HEAT AND COOLING CAPABILITIES (Be a snowbird and follow seasons.)

LIGHTS (Sun is the best lamp.)

PROVISIONS FOR COOKING (Ah, those campfire flapjacks!)

ITEMS FOR ENTERTAINMENT AND LEARNING
(Music systems, books)

PRIVACY, SECURITY AND COMMUNICATIONS EQUIPMENT.

Inasmuch as we mentioned a trailer being used as a hideout, let's see how the above essentials can be obtained from a modestly-priced, under 20-foot travel trailer, in this example, my own. The trailer provides space for shelter, storage of food, air, water and clothing. It also has a shower, toilet, bed, stove for heating and cooking, fan, 12-volt lights, a stereo system, books, locks on the doors, security via choice of location, and communications via the nearest pay phone. So, in a small space, just about everything needed to survive in comfort is available. Our point is clear. You don't really need much to enjoy your hideout.

Incidentally, just prior to writing this book I made two trips. One to Santa Fe, NM, and the other to EXPO '86 in Canada. The total mileage was about 7,000. The time involved was two months for both trips and yet there were almost no complaints from my better half, Ruth, who is a very fastidious person. This is proof that one can live quite simply and yet meet virtually every human need.

FOOD, AIR AND WATER

Hideouts imply storage, so foods like whole grains (wheat, corn, barley, rice), beans, nuts and seeds are most appropriate for long-term backup. Fortunately, these foods are inexpensive when purchased in bulk. A 100-lb sack of whole grain wheat sells for about $10. Beans have come down in price lately and I have seen them for as little as $18/100 lb. Some of the other storables that you might consider are popcorn, millet, lentils, alfalfa seeds (can be sprouted as can most other seeds), soybeans, flour, grits, honey, molasses, sunflower seeds (a most valuable source of vitamins and minerals), yeast (edible and baking) dry milk powder and dried herbs and spices. Note that sugar and salt are absent; the former is a drug and the latter will elevate your blood pressure.

With a plentiful supply of the above items, you can then add potatoes, onions, vegetables, fruits and lean meats as they are available to you. Don't forget that there are thousands of wild foods that can be foraged to embellish and enhance your daily diet.

Air quality has become a factor in health and there's no question that you will live a longer and more vigorous life if you opt for non-urban hideouts. Water is also a questionable item in almost any area, although the high-country streams fed by snow-melt are no doubt more pure than city tap water or rivers that collect farmland pesticide residues. When in doubt, try distilling your own water or buy purified water from a reliable source.

SHELTER

One can be in heaven curled up in a down sleeping bag cushioned by a foam pad in some wilderness paradise. Who needs a house or even a tent? Shelter options are limitless, as we imply in another chapter. How you live your life determines what you need in the way of shelter. Personally, I have found that the minimal shelter allows maximum freedom. And the smaller your shelter, the easier it is to conceal!

CLOTHING

This is a matter of personal choice and should be appropriate to your hideout locale and needs. I love camouflage suits for hiking in sylvan surroundings and birthday suits for lolling in primitive hot springs. For urban hideouts conservative dress is recommended to ensure a low profile. (So many people have been arrested just because they sported some outlandish and bizarre costume!!) As a general rule, dress according to your environment; sports outfits along the rivers, Mr. Straight garb when you are just driving around. You wouldn't put a 100,000 candlepower beacon on your hideout — why put the equivalent on your bod in the form of attention-getting clothing?

BATHING FACILITIES

One of the best attributes of many hideouts is that they are proximate to rivers, lakes and streams, if not a delightful hot spring! Thus, keeping clean can be as natural as a dip in the nearest watercourse. On the other hand, if you find water scarce, a sponge bath with some solar-heated water can keep you healthy and presentable. I have found the 2 1/2-gallon drinking water containers to be ideal for an outdoor shower. Just fill one with lukewarm water (or leave it in the sun for a few hours), hang it from a tree and enjoy!

SANITATION FACILITIES

While a toilet is usually an integral part of a trailer, motorhome or other RV, you might have to improvise in a wilderness setting. An old fashioned Chic Sale will work fine as long as you move it regularly to avoid buildup of contaminants. If you have only part-time occupancy of a hideout, try the latest, inexpensive portable toilets. Now coming on the market are some high-tech toilets that use heat to eliminate waste rather than flushing it away with gallons of water. Check home furnishing mags for addresses of suppliers.

COMFORTABLE BED

While there's an abundance of choices in either foam or air beds, think about the fragrance of fresh hay or straw or the resiliency of balsam boughs. The natural beds are around for the taking and can be easily replaced. I often think of the Santa Barbara backcountry days when I spent the late afternoon gathering a mound of wild oats for a most restful sleep under the stars.

HEAT AND COOLING CAPABILITIES

My own vision of a hideout is one that takes advantage of the ambient climate. This would imply that you really need a place in Montana's mountains in the summer and a sunny spot near the Mexican border in winter. However, if you intend to tough it out against heat and cold here are some suggestions. Modern, air-tight, cast iron stoves use only a small amount of wood to keep your hideout snug. You can also insert a coil of tubing to heat your bath water. My choice for cooling is the evaporative cooler that requires only water and some means of circulating the air. You can build one from a simple metal or even wood box, some wood shavings and two motors, one to recirculate the water and the other to move the air. If where you are has steady breezes, you can possibly skip the latter. The Egyptians used large panels of loosely woven cloth through which water dripped and air blew. It worked great for them and it can for you.

LIGHTS

Here the range is from the old reliable kerosene lantern (Aladdins are very efficient) to the high-tech solar-powered, low-voltage, fluorescent. There is an interesting alternative to artificial lights — try the natural way and read by daylight, study the clouds and stars after the sun goes down. Might improve your eyesight and your perceptions.

PROVISIONS FOR COOKING

During the Great Depression of the '30's a very popular stove was made from a standard kerosene lantern. The top was removed and a grill of heavy wire substituted. Now one could put a pot containing whatever was around...spuds, vegies, a soup bone and some barley plus water...in place and let the slow flame "crock pot" a delicious meal. This plus outdoor cooking can greatly simplify and economize on cooking equipment. Also, it's becoming well-known that we need to eat more raw foods, perhaps as much as 80 percent of our diet. After all, when you heat anything above about 130 F, you kill off the enzymes which are needed in the digestion process. Ever see a lion or tiger barbecue their evening chow? Or a mighty goose simmer her corn or greens? Q.E.D.

ENTERTAINMENT AND LEARNING

Thanks to the proliferation of 12-volt DC equipment, it's possible to enjoy just about anything that high-tech electronics offers in your remotest of hideouts. From a simple compact disk player to a satellite receiver for worldwide TV programs, it's all available to install anywhere you choose. And you can power it with photovoltaics, hydro or wind.

If a source of mail service or UPS is handy, then the world of learning via books can embellish your hideout life. Most publishers offer their wares by mail and some make an exclusive business of this mode of marketing, Loompanics for instance.

Thus, you need lack for nothing in the way of cultural experiences. You can enjoy Mozart or Linda Ronstadt while reading London and Proust no matter where you choose to establish your privacy domain.

PRIVACY, SECURITY AND COMMUNICATIONS EQUIPMENT

Again, high-tech electronics, particularly solid-state, offers a cornucopia of goodies to make your hideout secret and safe. Here are just a few examples from the many offered, many by mail for your convenience.

When you travel from Hideout A in the redwoods of Mendocino County in California to Hideout B in downtown Carmel, you'll find this ETAK Navigator Model 450 with the 4.5 inch screen quite handy. It will provide you with the most direct route as well as all alternates. It's the Loran of the highways! More info on Etak? Phone (425) 328-3825

Electrical Independence Booklets

BY DAVID COPPERFIELD

THESE SMALL PAMPHLETS ARE FULL OF VALUABLE DO-IT-YOURSELF INSTRUCTIONS, PACKED INTO VERY FEW PAGES.

THE SUN AND WHEELS POWER SYSTEM: Here's the inexpensive way to get started with independent power. Overview of solar-electric system with dual battery back-up. Typical appliances for various sized systems. Buyer's guide, charts, and more.

HOW TO INSTALL SOLAR ELECTRIC PANELS: Do it right for optimum power. Sizing your system for year-round reliability. Mounting designs for wind or snow conditions. Roof, wall, pole, and tree mounts. Wiring schematics. Battery sizing and care. Monitors, voltage regulators, and more.

HOW TO INSTALL A TWO BATTERY SYSTEM IN YOUR VEHICLE: Complete instructions for this handy back-up system includes information on isolators, monitors, and how to wire for fast charging or automatic jumper cables.

BUILD YOUR OWN SMALL POWER PLANT: An inexpensive back-up system that fast-charges batteries, runs small power tools, and even does light-duty welding. Uses a common lawn mower engine and car alternator. Step-by-step instructions and illustrations.

BUILD YOUR OWN SOLAR ELECTRIC PANEL: Step-by-step instructions with clear illustrations for the do-it-yourselfer. List of materials, tools and sources for cells.

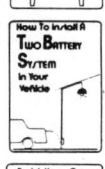

ALL ABOUT INVERTERS: Here's how to run lots of AC appliances in your 12v home, and for little cost. Inverter sizes and efficiency. How to avoid inverter "burn-out". How to install remote switching, wiring for both AC and DC.

GETTING THE MOST FROM YOUR BATTERIES: Learn what kind of battery best suits your system and how many you'll need. Optimal charge and discharge rates. Proper storage and venting. Maintenance. Buyer's guide, charts, and plenty of eye-opening information.

CONVERT YOUR WRINGER WASHER TO 12 VOLTS: Now you can convert one of the simplest and best types of washers ever made. Every step explained and illustrated. Includes instructions for adding a timer for extra convenience.

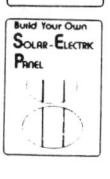

BUILD A 12 VOLT NiCad BATTERY CHARGER: Recharge NiCad flashlight batteries up to 1000 times with this easy-to-build device. Complete instructions with good illustrations. Usual and unusual appliances NiCads will run.

HOW TO CONVERT TURNTABLES TO 12 VOLTS: Every step explained and illustrated making it easy to modify available turntables and cassette decks. List of easiest models to convert, and sources for 12v amplifiers. (56)

CONVERT AUTOMATIC WASHERS TO 12 VOLTS: Imagine the convenience of automatic washing in your electrically-independent home! Step-by-step instructions with plenty of illustrations. Complete list of parts and tools. Sources for 12 volt motors.

CONVERT DRYERS TO 12 VOLT: Gas or electric can be converted through use of propane or wood stove for heat. How to install 12v tumbler motor and power timer and solenoids.

HOW TO PUMP WATER WITH SOLAR ELECTRICITY: Deep wells, shallow wells, streams, ponds, or springs. Pressurizing systems. Sizing. Choosing the right pump and motor. Wiring, charts. Sources.

12 VOLT APPLIANCES: Discover the many appliances you can run, where to get them, their cost, and their power draw. Strategies for running almost any appliance. Conversions. Sources.

THE 12 VOLT SHOP: Tools for every job and how to run them with a 12 volt system. Sources for major tools without AC motors (save). Buy little known 12v tools (sources) Tools that can be run on an inexpensive inverter. One 12v motor for many tools. Wiring. Sources.

Write to ALTERNATIVE ENERGY ENGINEERING, PO 339, REDWAY, CA 95560 for more information on these booklets and hardware.

INFRA-RED (IR) HUMAN SENSORS

Passive Infra-Red Intruder Sensors

• A new intruder detector now being widely used is the infra-red passive sensor. Patterned after highly sophisticated military IR (infra-red) sensors, the new units will detect and sound the alarm when a person moves into the area which is protected. Unlike micro and ultra-sonic detectors they are passive. (do not radiate energy).

• IR sensors consist of an extremely sensitive crystal assembly that senses the difference between the infra-red radiation of a human body entering the protected area and the air temperature in the room or outdoors. This differential sensing circuit will cause a sensitive relay to operate and "trip" an alarm panel or any lock-up power relay connected to the IR sensor.

• These IR units require a 6 or 12 volt DC source and current of 10-20 milliamperes. This current can be supplied from most existing control panels. Some of the units listed on this page will work on a low cost 6.0-volt lantern battery with an expected battery life up to 1-year.

• The relationship of the infra-red sensors and the alarm system is shown in Fig. 1. You will note that these sensors are not an alarm system in themselves, but rather a slave actuator which feeds a trip signal to the alarm panel, causing the panel to "lock-up" and sound the alarm.

Figure 1

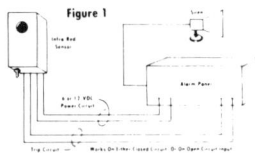

INFRA-RED INTRUSION DETECTOR
Model 9435

ITEM 29-J-005

$119.95

INFRA-RED INTRUSION SENSOR
(Model 5020)

ITEM 29-J-003

$143.95

• **ITEM 29-J-003** - - The model 5020 sensor is designed to protect large rooms in homes, high risk areas in commercial buildings such as a gun or camera department in a sporting goods store, computer installation in a business office, etc. This unit has an effective range of 50' x 20' with a vertical spread of 6' at maximum range.

• An LED test light on the front of the sensor comes ON when anyone enters or goes through the protected area. The light remains ON while the movement is taking place. After the movement stops the light goes OFF and the sensor automatically resets itself. When the LED light first comes ON the control panel locks up and sounds the alarm. The output relay terminals permit either closed circuit or open circuit output.

• The unit can be powered by either 6 or 12-VDC at 15 to 30-MA which can usually be obtained from the security lock-up control panel. The mounting bracket furnished permits easy mounting on a flat wall or in a corner. Inexpensive 4-wire #22-gauge cable can be used to connect the infra-red sensor to the control panel or to a simple lock-up module.

• Overall size 5-1/2" x 3" x 1-1/2". Shipping weight 3 lbs.

• **ITEM 29-J-005** - - This unit represents the latest advancements in passive infra-red technology. Designed for flat surface hardware installation on walls or in corners. It provides an intrusion protection area of 35 ft. long by 20 ft. wide. The sensing element is adjustable vertically and horizontally for optimum coverage of the protected area. Sensitivity is also adjustable. When the protected area is intruded the relay contacts switch to the alarm condition and will remain in this mode for 10-seconds after the intruder has left.

• Operates on 6 to 18-VDC. Current consumption is 40-MA on 12-VDC. Power can be supplied by a control panel or battery. Has built-in LED walk test indicator. Relay contacts can be used either NO or NC. Overall size 7-1/4" x 4" x 1-5/8". Shpg. wt. 1 lb.

RECESSED INFRA-RED SENSOR
(Recessed Enclosure)

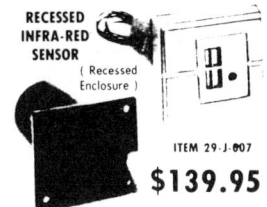

ITEM 29-J-007

$139.95

• **ITEM 29-J-007** - - Mounts in 2" diameter hole. Very compact yet provides coverage up to 20' x 40'. Sensitivity adjustment for optimum coverage.

• Operates on 6 to 18-VDC from control panel or seperate power supply. Low 15-Ma current draw. Built-in walk test LED. Contacts may be used as either N.O. or N.C. Size: 3-1/2" x 3" x 2-3/4". Wt. 1 lb.

OUTSIDE ENTRANCE INFRA-RED SENSOR

Model 4025

$149.50
6" x 4" x 2"
Shpg. wt. 4 lbs.

• **ITEM 29-J-006** - - Automatically turns on outside entrance lights whenever anyone enters the field of the infra-red sensor. Provides a safe, lighted entrance for the family, for your guests and serves to ward off any intruders trying to work under the cover of darkness. Its an energy saver too since you don't need to leave your lights on continuously when you are away from home. Lights turn off automatically after pre-set time (adjustable 10-seconds to 20-minutes) if the protected area is vacated.

• Protects an area up to 40' x 25'. Infra-red radiation from a human body entering the area trips a relay which switches on the lights connected to the unit. Operates on 115-VAC and will handle up to 500-watts. Has focusing and sensitivity adjustments. Photoswitch automatically deactivates the unit during daylight periods. Can also be used to trip remote alarm panels.

• **NOTE:** We can furnish an AC auxiliary relay for operating remote alarm panels, bells, etc. for the Model 4025 sensor for only **$1.95**.

Space Protection Devices

Drive Alert Vehicle Sensor

PROTECTS:
- Residential/Home
- Farm
- Business
- Factory

• Provides detection of out-of-sight vehicles on driveways. Sensor detects change in earth's magnetic field caused by a passing vehicle. Will detect moving metal objects in a radius up to 15-feet and transmit a signal to a control panel equipped with a built-in audible signal.

• Both sensor and cable are buried approximately 6" underground. Unit is furnished with 100 ft. of direct burial cable but sensor can be mounted up to 5000 ft. from control by adding extra cable. More flexibility can also be gained by adding one or two additional sensors to system.

• Electronic whistle sounds as vehicle passes by. Control also has a built-in relay to turn on lights, trigger control panel, etc. Unit works off 115-VAC and feature s adjustable sensitivity.

• **ITEM 29-B-031** — Standard outfit of control panel, 100 ft burial cable and sensor Wt 6 lbs
$179.95

• **ITEM 29-H-021** — Extra cable for extending distance from control to sensor Minimum order 50 ft
26c/Ft.

• **ITEM 29-B-032** — Extra sensor for coverage in second area. Supplied with 100 ft of cable. Wt 2 lbs
$59.95

FEATURES:
- Sensor completely hidden
- Electronic whistle
- Whistle time adjustable
- Sensitivity range adjustable
- Solid state sensor
- Easy installation

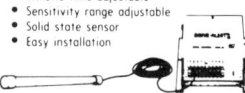

Photoelectric Intrusion Detector

$115.95   Shpg. wt. 1 lb.

• **ITEM 29-B-030** — These units operate on the time proven idea of detecting an intruder breaking a light beam. Since they employ pulsed infrared light, the beam is not visible to the human eye.

• Outfit consists of a transmitter and receiver mounted at either end of the protected space. Each portion operates off 12-VDC which can be supplied by the control panel or a separate power source. The relay contacts in the receiver activate when the beam is interrupted.

• Small size of the units make them almost unnoticeable. Mounting bracket allows adjustment over 180° range. A walk test light is included in the receiver.

• While detection occurs only in a straight line path between units, the wide transmitter beam allows multiple receiver for added coverage.

_____ **Specifications** _____

Range 150 ft
Relay output S.P.D.T. (normally open or closed)
Size: Transmitter 2-1/2" x 2-1/3" x 1-1/3"
       Receiver 2-1/2" x 3-3/4" x 1-1/2"
Power Consumption on 12-VDC
       Transmitter 75 Ma
       Receiver 45 Ma

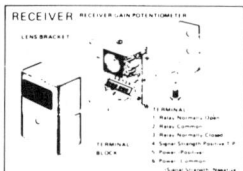

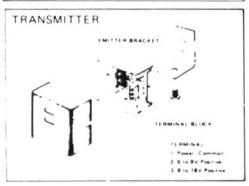

Microwave Sensors

• Latest design motion detector uses a microwave transceiver to provide space protection. Shielding and filtering eliminate problems from radio interference and flourescent lighting. These sensors are very stable over time and wide temperature variations. All metal enclosure for additional false signal rejection.

• Electronic circuit of sensor draws only 15 Ma which allows it to be powered from control panel, even during standby battery operation. This is possible due to pulsed output which greatly reduces power consumption.

• Dual walk test lights for ease of installation. Lights can be disabled to prevent intruders testing of the covered area. Separate range and sensitivity controls to adjust unit for most precise operation. Contacts may be set as either N.O. or N.C. Rated for 2 amps.

• Operates on 12-VDC from control panel or auxillary power back. Furnished with swivel hinge and bracket. Size 3" x 3-1 2" x 5-3 4". Shipping wt. 4 lbs

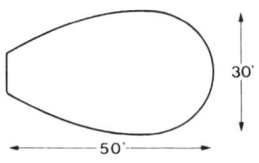

• **ITEM 29-B-034** — Coverage Pattern 30' x 50'
$149.50

• **ITEM 29-B-035** — Coverage Pattern 30' x 120'
$179.95

TYPES OF HIDEOUTS

What kinds of hideouts are suitable for Western application? With so many varieties of terrain available it's obvious that there must be an equal variety or selection in the actual hideout facility. No way is your camper/trailer rig going to navigate Georgia Strait, at least not without pontoons. And that beautifully maintained Chris Craft would be like the proverbial waterless fish if it tried navigating the dunes of White Sands.

Herewith, then, a review of hideouts from the most visionary, existing only in the mind, to a sturdy log hut in the northern wilds of Washington.

THE HIDEOUT PLAN

This one costs little but may save a lot, your life and the lives of your family. It consists of a plan that would go into action when necessary. An example will make it clear.

Let's assume that you live in an area where earthquakes are common. The coastal region where I live is typical since I'm not far from the San Andreas fault. You select an inland area to which you can retreat in the event that California tilts and begins sliding into the vast Pacific. Assuming that you can make it out of town in time, you head for the selected hideout location. It might be a favorite resort, a hot springs or the home of a friend. Assuming that you have a little money saved up, you can restart your life in the new location, using your temporary hideout as a base.

Plans of this type can be infinitely varied. Some can be merely locations on a map; others can be definite arrangements to move into an old mining claim owned by a friend. Or, assuming that you can get away in time, the plan can include a camper, trailer, motorhome or other type of RV that you would use for your escape.

THE RV HIDEOUT

Fortunately, the vacation-loving American public has generated millions of new and used RV's. Many of them can be purchased quite reasonably, and equipped to suit your needs and stocked with enough supplies to make a transition.

I have always assumed that many RV owners had this contingency in mind when they bought their rigs. The presence of a reliable camper with the tanks filled not only gives a feeling of assurance to the owner, it is probably the best *insurance* against disastrous happenings.

One of the greatest benefits of the mobile hideout is that it can be located almost anywhere, assuming, of course, that roads remain in drivable condition. Another option is to purchase an inexpensive RV and pre-locate it in a desired hideout area. Now you have the problem of reaching it, but at least it's already *there*.

THE FANTASY CABIN

Discuss hideouts, and most often the picture of a small but sturdy log cabin in some pristine forest is evoked. This can, of course, be a reality. Wilderness land can be acquired, often at low cost. A chain saw is really all that is needed to fell, trim and fabricate logs into a traditional structure. Basic utilities can consist of piped spring water, a dug well or even a tank you fill with hauled-in water. Heat and cooking can be pioneer style, a big black pot swinging over the native stone fireplace. Bunks with straw mattresses will provide expandable accommodations while supplies such as beans and rice can be stored in metal cans tucked away in odd corners. If building and stocking a cabin is not on your time schedule, then it's always possible to buy one ready-made.

SOME MISCELLANEOUS OPTIONS FOR YOUR HIDEOUT

The Totally Hidden Underground Hideout

Beloved by pre-teen boys, the excavated cave covered by natural foliage can be as simple as a one-room "bomb shelter" or an elaborate labyrinth of subterranean rooms resembling the famous underground gardens in Fresno. Modern earth-surrounded technology has made below grade houses a most feasible, practical and sensible option for either full- or part-time living. Best of all, if you take pains to camouflage the entrance and any utility connections, you'll never have to worry about visitors!

Tree Houses

The foundation of a house is one of the most massive undertakings in its construction. If you can eliminate it in some way, you are way ahead, and that's what happens when you use a tree as a base. Scattered all over the world are examples of tree houses, some simply for play, others for real. Not far from where I live there are fanciful tree dwellings with all utilities and so well-hidden that you couldn't find them without a map or instructions. One important point is to build flexibly to allow for tree movement and growth.

The Warehouse

Increasingly popular as both hideouts and cheap places to live are the many converted industrial buildings that festoon wharves and low-income neighborhoods. I've personally visited a number of beautifully decorated warehouse conversions that resembled Park Avenue penthouses. One was the home/studio of a professional and successful artist who loved the drama and romance of living in an otherwise rejected and seedy part of town. His wonderful paintings (Rembrandt replicas using cartoon character heads) covered the walls and gave the entire facility an Arabian Nights fantasy overlay.

Barns

In rural areas it is often possible to acquire a large old barn or shed which can then be converted to a hideout of any desired degree of comfort and convenience. I recall finding a Nob Hill-type apartment *inside* a former hay barn. Even if you walked into the barn itself, the apartment area was still hidden behind walls of old boards. But once inside — presto-chango — a magnificent, self-contained, all-in-one-room luxury home!

Mines

Scattered all over the west are tens of thousands of mines, mining claims, mill sites and other activities and facilities related to obtaining valuable minerals. A percentage of these would make ideal hideouts since many have developed utilities (water, electricity, sanitation and even food-growing capability). You can buy or lease a mine or mining claim, often quite reasonably. It is legal to live on a mine claim as long as you are performing at least $100 worth of work per year (a stipulation that has not changed since the mining act of 1870 was ratified). I have always believed that having a hideout combined with a potential income (gold is over $300 an ounce) would be one of the ideal ways to enjoy both privacy and economic independence.

Ghost Towns

Another Western feature is the existence of thousands of abandoned towns in almost every state. And don't forget the large numbers of long-forgotten lumber camps in heavily forested states like Oregon and Washington. These tumble-down communities offer unlimited potential to hideout seekers in that many of them are far from active road systems, bureaucratic enclaves or nosy neighbors. I've found people living in restored dwellings in such diverse locations as northern Oregon and the Panamint Valley of California.

River Islands

Few people are aware that the tens of thousands of small, sandy islands and islets that are present in many river systems have no real legal status. Because they can be over-run by a flooding river, no one really wants to claim them or pay taxes. Consequently, these parcels of land can be used by anyone who is willing to take a risk of having a wet winter destroy or damage their dwelling. To this day, people live on quite safe islands in the California Delta and I found an entire village of free-thinkers growing all their own food on an acre-sized parcel in the middle of the great Salmon River in Idaho. What would be advisable for these tenuous parcels would be tent-like structures that could be folded up and removed at the first sign of aquatic disaster. Questionable security, but the price is certainly right!

Silos and Other Farm Storage Buildings

As farming in America descends into an economic abyss, thousands of the familiar round silos become available for other uses. I have seen conversions of these and large water tanks into suitable hideout homes. They can be used where you find them or moved to more appropriate locales. Sturdy and long-lasting, they make perfect shells for creative homes that have their camouflage as an inherent characteristic. On the slope of a hill overlooking Bolinas is a most charming water-tank-house and nearby is another made from an old wine cask. The possibilities are endless and, again, the price can be more than right.

Abandoned Boats on Land

Floating hideouts are described in another part of this book but don't forget the possibilities of having a cozy hideout inside a vessel that is safely parked on dry land. In Moss Landing, California, I know of a man my age who enjoys rent-free living in an old WWII landing craft stored in a boat yard. It's a legal arrangement since he functions as a night watchman and uses the boat yard sanitary facilities, including a hot shower. As the fishing industry moves overseas, there are more and more old fishing boats parked on empty lots in maritime communities. Play it cool, keep the windows curtained at night and you can enjoy a compact, unsinkable home for peanuts. If any hassles do occur, one can always give a story about "fixing up the boat for later use."

Gas Stations

Every year there are fewer of the old-fashioned, we-serve-you gas stations in America. The modern serve-yourself with a cashier in a bullet-proof kiosk is the late 20th century mode of petrol merchandising. Consequently, one can often buy or lease a station, particularly in towns that have been bypassed by freeway systems. These can be converted to comfortable dwellings since they already have the necessary utilities. One conversion includes the use of an old grease pit as a hot tub. Leave the exterior "as-is" but build what you wish inside. In that way you can retain the abandoned facade and be assured of a hassle-free hideout.

Old Hotels and Motels

Things are changing rapidly in the highway accommodations field. Many motels and hotels are being abandoned because they have been victims of both

Inn or Resort, call toll free anytime

technological advances and highway rerouting. More people use RV's and more freeways leave towns to decline. Again, there are many opportunities to acquire properties of this type and remodel to suit your individual needs. How many times have you noticed old hotels with boarded up windows that were still obviously being used as domiciles? And the same is true of motels in formerly busy highway service towns.

A good source of information about these hideouts-to-be would be local realty firms as well as United Farm Agency which publishes a large catalog. Write United at 612 W 47th St., Kansas City, MO 64112 for a free copy of their latest rural property listings.

Want to know which towns are going to become ghosts? Then get in touch with the highway department in your state and ask for a copy of their plans for future freeway routing. It's public knowledge and should be free for the asking. If not, write the governor.

Caves

Near Lone Pine, California, there is a low bluff of soft rock. Centuries ago, Indians aided the wind in carving caves. Today most are occupied by tough old pensioners who survive on laughable social security checks and the fresh dry air that is the health-preserving agent in this region. Although a cave may seem primitive to the uninitiated, they are used widely throughout the world as full-time living quarters. If you want to see some sophisticated cave dwellings, visit the Indian country near where four states (Utah, Colorado, Arizona, New Mexico) join their boundaries. Not far from Four Corners is the legendary Mesa Verde National Park which will prove that living in caves can be both frugal and comfortable not to mention private.

Tents

Modern fabrics made of man-made materials have radically changed the tent scene. Today you can buy a tent of any size that can be erected and then stored in minutes. This capability makes the instant hideout in almost any location a viable reality. Imagine selecting just the place that fits your immediate but temporary needs, setting up a livable and comfortable tent-house and then being able to move in less time than it takes to hitch up a trailer! Also, modern camping equipment, with its below-zero-withstanding sleeping bags and clothing, light-weight stoves and freeze-dried foods, adds to the "instant hideout" possibilities.

THE IDEAL GETAWAY

No. 349— 4 1/2 acres, $15,000. Inviting 4 1/2-acre parcel offers building site amid trees in peaceful and tranquil setting. Only 1/2 mile to fishing river, approximately 30 minutes to national forest and wilderness areas. 5 miles to town. Perfect for privacy seekers at $15,000, low down payment, owner financing at 10% annual percentage rate. *Redmond, Oreg.*

LONE WOLF'S FARMSTEAD

No. 2492— 20 acres, $34,000. Enjoy utmost seclusion within shouting distance of the Canadian border. Hidden 2 room log cabin, barn, root cellar, auxiliary generator and photovoltaic system. Small family orchard, garden area. Gravity flow spring water. 20 acres, 17 acres wooded. Solar panel, wood heating and cook stoves, refrigerator, more included. Be one with nature for $34,000, owner financing at 9 1/2% annual percentage rate. Discount for cash. *Colville, Wash.*

RANCHLAND VALUE $200 PER ACRE!

No. 795— 800 acres, $160,000. Price has been slashed on this remote ranchland mostly surrounded by federal lands. 800 acres in 2 parcels, one 640 and another 160 acres, 80 tillable with 20 irrigated. Year-round creek presently provides stock water for 2,000 sheep and 35 horses, could irrigate more land. Owner has planted 400 grapevines. Very secluded setting at base of cliffs, 8 miles to Interstate, short drive town. Reduced to only

$160,000, good owner financing at 10% annual percentage rate. *Moab, Utah.*

A few selections of hideout-type property from the United Farm Agency Catalog.

SECLUDED MOUNTAIN LAND

No. 956— 78 acres, $43,000. Wonderful location to develop your mountain ranch or recreational paradise! 78 acres, 15 improved pasture, 50 wooded, including ponderosa pine, well. Old adobe building could be used for animal shelter. Short drive to town, lake. $43,000, assumable loan to qualified buyer. *Colorado City, Colo.*

REMOTE 1,280-ACRE RANCH INDIAN RUINS, BLUFFS!

No. 102— 1,280 acres, $300,000. Scenic sandstone bluffs (many with ancient pictographs), lots of trees and productive grasses on beautiful 1,280-acre ranch. Approximately 500 tillable acres with 300 in improved pasture. Indian artifacts found throughout ranch. Additional 640 acres state leased land included. 4 wells, 2 ponds, fenced and cross fenced. Complete privacy at end of county maintained road, 60 miles Gallup. Older set of improvements need repair. Come see the unusual for $300,000, loan assumption to qualified buyer. *Quemado, N. Mex.*

HUNTER'S HIDEAWAY

No. 251— 120 acres, $77,000. Secluded 120-acre tract along the scenic North Fork of John Day River offers good hunting and fishing. Spacious 3-bedroom lodge only 5 years old, paneling, wood heat. Smokehouse, rabbit hutches. Rim rocks, open spaces, plus timbered draws make for excellent late season elk hunting while steelhead make their way up the river. Springs. Public access to property, 15 miles town. $77,000, $15,000 down, long-term owner financing at 10% annual percentage rate. *John Day-Prairie City, Oreg.*

FIX-UP MOUNTAIN ESCAPE

No. 816— 15 acres, $35,000. Fifteen acres of forest seclusion and an unfinished cabin to finish— includes materials to finish. Has good roof, floor and exterior walls. Spring supplies domestic water through gravity flow system. Excellent all-year creek, excellent mountain views. Forest service land on 2 sides. Be one with nature for only $35,000. *Eagle Point, Oreg.*

HORSE RANCH HIDEAWAY

No. 2503— 28 acres, $100,000. Creek-crossed ranchette makes the perfect place for raising your prize horses. 28 acres, fenced meadow with creek running through to feed large pond, 5 acres seeded to alfalfa. Stately remodeled home exudes old-time country charm, has 5 bedrooms, 2 baths, bay windows, enclosed porch. 40x50-ft. 2-story barn, storage shed with smokehouse, garage. Picturesque and secluded setting, yet with paved road frontage, only 1 mile to town. Lucky find for the horse fancier at $100,000. *Colville, Wash.*

STONE CABIN IN WOODS

No. 114— $25,000. Rustic stone cabin with rippling creek 20 ft. from back porch. Has bedroom, bath, equipped kitchen, fireplace. Comes with furnishings and gold panning equipment included. On 1 acre of BLM land. 2 miles to town. Enjoy the secluded country life at $25,000. *Mesa, Ariz.*

Real estate prices are on their way down in many areas. However, if a hideout location is still beyond your budget, consider sharing a parcel with another privacy seeker.

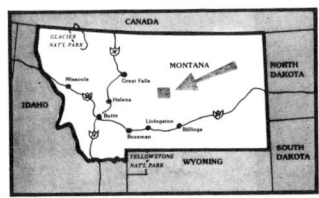

Flat Willow Creek Ranch
Code: "FW"

Location: 35 miles southeast of Lewistown, Montana in the "Little Snowy" Mountain Range. About 50 miles north and west of Roundup, Montana. Flat Willow Creek, a great trout fishing stream runs thru this property. Access is by a maintained county road which parallels the creek. <u>Here is a place with almost no one else around.</u> Year around access is a strong possibility.

General Description

Located about 35 miles southeast of Lewistown, Montana the Flat Willow Creek Ranch is a beautiful grassy valley about ¼ to ½ mile wide, surrounded by rolling to broken lower mountain terrain covered with pine trees and an occasional pocket of light green aspen trees. Flat Willow Creek itself winds its way along the valley floor, and is a beautiful fishing stream! Mule deer and whitetail deer are often seen watering in or browsing along the creek. Even though you are miles from the nearest town the county does plow and maintain the main road through the ranch which parallels the creek, so year around living or winter access would be possible here.

At this writing we are just completing the purchase of this beautiful ranch. We hope to have it on the market by early summer. We expect the prices to run from $12,500. for 20 acres, that's a piece in the rougher high country, to the $19,000. to $27,000. range along the creek and county road.

When you stop by to see us this summer make sure to ask about this one as we will be ready to give someone first pick of this property soon!

Photos taken on Flat Willow Creek Ranch

Proof that people are seeking remote property is provided by the fact that the company offering the land on this and the next page has expanded rapidly. For information call Yellowstone Basin Properties, 1-800-252-LAND.

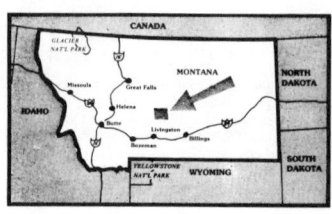

Smeller Lake
Code: "SML"

Location: At the south end of the Crazy Mountain Range near Crazy Peak. Also located at the east end of Rock Creek drainage. Smeller Lake, approximately 40 acres in size is located on this property. **Nearest road access 7 miles away. Access by backpacking, horseback or helicopter only! Extremely Remote.**

General Description <u>Author's emphasis</u>

This property consists of 640 acres located high in the Crazy Mountains. Our land is surrounded on all sides by National Forest and is accessible by trail or helicopter only! The nearest road is about seven miles from Smeller Lake and a couple of thousand feet lower in elevation. Smeller Lake itself is about 40 acres in size and is a great lake for high mountain trout fishing.

For those of you who are looking for an extremely remote place to go, whether to hunt, photograph or just kick back for awhile, I suggest you request further information. This is where you find the "really big" big game. The old smart ones hang out here. Mountain goats, bear, elk and mule deer are abundant around Smeller Lake. There are also several other high mountain lakes near our property that are on adjoining national forest land. Our plan at this time is to set aside about 100 acres around the lake and build a small cabin on it. Since most of the balance of the land is extremely steep, we do not plan to survey the lot corners. Each purchaser will own 20 acres but we are assuming the primary reason for purchasing will be to have use of the cabin and the 100 acre lake area. Price per 20 acre parcel is $9,950. with $250. down and $137.77 per month.

20 Acres $9,950.   Min. Down $250.   Mo. Pmt. $137.77

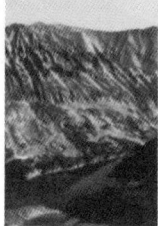  

All photos taken on Smeller Lake property or on adjoining national forest.

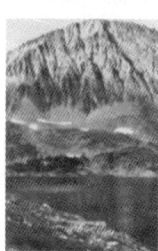  

Farms and Ranches

Today, the trend is to make big farms out of little ones, but in the process, lots of little ones are left behind. You see, many original homesteads are in remote locations, have iffy water supplies and are cut up so that amalgamation is difficult. Consequently, they are both almost unsalable and imposssible to integrate with a larger operation. If you read the pages of various farm realty catalogs you'll find many farms listed outright as "abandoned." This same predicament has visited many of the old time ranches along with the current declining demand for beef.

The upshot is that you can obtain rural land for much less than it would have cost only a few years ago. In addition, where an abandoned property is concerned, you might be able to acquire it for very little, on a lease or through barter of some tangibles.

My own fantasy of a farm hideout is to forget the main house. Let it appear to be reverting to nature and then occupy one of the usual outbuildings. One of my close friends has a farm of this nature and has the barn full of esoteric, brain-feed-back electronics. No one is ever the wiser!

So if you need space for a project, consider one of the thousands of rural properties that will come on the market in the next few years.

Attics and Cellars

Virtually all homes have structural shapes which provide space directly beneath the roof. These attic areas are seldom used but certainly could be. I have often visualized the use of an attic as the real dwelling place of an avid hideouter while the so-called main rooms can be given over to the use of friends or relatives. Judicious use of the available headroom would provide walkways while all activities such as dining or sleeping can be accommodated along the lower elevations. Modern air-conditioning and lighting would take care of these needs. And with contemporary electronics there would be no need to feel shut off from the mainstream. Microwave links, modems, and computers would permit almost any type of enterprise, and all from an unseen and unvisited base!

The same benefits would be gained by excavating a large cellar beneath a dwelling. It might require a jackhammer to get through the slab but the same monolithic chunk of concrete would provide a waterproof and strong "roof." You might study the trench systems of WWI to get an idea of how extensively one can build sub-surface. Best of all, other than labor and some materials, there would be no further cost of real estate, insurance or taxes.

Nurseries and Greenhouses

One of the best hideout facilities in my opinion would be the multiple use of a greenhouse or nursery. By their very nature they are seldom visited, particularly if they are the type that simply grows plants and flowers for marketing elsewhere. To me, horticulture would be a great cover for a very private lifestyle. One's living quarters could be concealed in any of the storage buildings. Imagine a floor to ceiling stack of potted soil sacks. Behind them is the secret entrance to your ultra-private hideout. Or imagine a greenhouse with hydroponically-grown, jungle-type plants that screen whatever facilities you want screened. Below-ground-level quarters and storage are also feasible since there are such things as mushroom cellars. It's just that there is that extra one that no one notices behind a stack of mushroom culture trays. I'm sure you get the picture.

"Official" Trailers and Other Mobile Dwellings

To this day I do not really know whether that green trailer with the U.S. GOVERNMENT PROPERTY sticker was really what it purported to be or whether it was some clever forest dweller's private home. But that's exactly why this mode of hideout could be one of the most successful. It seems that someone placed a rather large park-model trailer in the remote back country of Santa Barbara (Los Padres National Forest). It remained there for many years, apparently unused. With its formidable sign: WARNING, TEN YEARS IN PRISON FOR MESSING...etc., it was safe from vandalism. But as mentioned, who put it there and why? Was it *really* a government outpost or merely the private home of some wag who bought an old trailer, painted it green and had a fine vacation hideout.

This thought presents many ramifications. It is completely feasible to purchase a trailer, motorhome, boat or truck and paint it in "official" colors. Then by adding appropriate signs and warnings, place it almost anywhere for free space and untroubled tenure. Imagine stenciling on the dreaded logo of the nuclear energy people with large WARNING, DEADLY RADIATION, KEEP OUT signs festooning the nearby trees. With Three-Mile Island and Chernobyl still in the public consciousness, I am quite certain that no one would bother your rig.

As a precaution, you could also leave an "official" number, which could be an answering service instructed to respond as any agency you wished to simulate.

The same success could be obtained by buying an old government vessel, painting it solemn gray and then adding some real or spurious government logos or symbols. You can let your imagination roam and come up with some new agencies such as:

FEDERAL CUSTOMS INVESTIGATION TASK FORCE

U.S. CENTRAL RESEARCH FACILITY

STATE OF NEVADA CUSTOMS EXAMINATION BOARD

Yes, to my mind, becoming "official" would be a great way to ensure the tranquility of your on-land or at-sea hideout, permanent or mobile.

A FEW HIDEOUT SCENARIOS

AN ALTERNATIVE TO BANKRUPTCY

The Nelsons were a typical American family. They had a new home, two cars, an accordion pleat of credit cards at least a yard long and debts that would ensure their economic slavery for at least the next thirty years.

Everything went along great until Reg Nelson was suddenly laid off from his $50,000-a-year job. Try as hard as he might, he could not find a similar position in his area. Before the month was up things began going back to the stores; the VCR, one of the cars, his wife's new washer and dryer. Then the house went into foreclosure forcing Reg and his wife to think seriously about where they and their two children were going to live. As one economic disaster followed another, the only out seemed to be bankruptcy, which the Nelsons could not accept. The alternative was to simply give up all their possessions and start over again from scratch. They had done it once and felt they could do it again.

But with one big difference. Reg decided that he wouldn't abide by the corporate imperatives this time. Instead he would find another way of life, an escape from the steely clutch of daily economics. Thus, with the very last of their money, the family bought bus tickets to a small coastal town in southern Washington. Clutching their suitcases they approached the only building showing lights, a well-kept Victorian hotel. Reg explained their monetary predicament to the owner-manager who, it just happened, operated his facility on a "share the wealth" basis. His staff received room and board and other necessities, and at the end of the month all profits were divided in an equitable manner.

Reg and his wife and children became night manager, cook's helper and room attendants in that order. When they bedded down in their comfortable suite they realized that the concept of an economic "hideout" was not only real, it could promise to be fun too!

PLAYING GAMES WITH THE IRS

Martin "Red" Condon is an avowed tax rebel. For the past 15 years he has devoted full time to writing about and publicizing the unconstitutional excesses of the Internal Revenue Service. Many of his friends are engaged in the same battle and some of them have gone to prison after the usual mock trial. Condon says that he is more effective outside than inside and thus has developed a chain of hideouts which, to date, have been the key to his elusiveness. He knows from having contacts inside the IRS that they would love to imprison him for a long term but so far have been failures at apprehending him.

The hideout chain is scattered all over the 11 Western states, some in cities, others in remote regions. One of his city locations is the attic of a friend's house where he has a typewriter, copy machine and other tools of his writing trade. Sometimes he arrives on foot wearing the coveralls of a tradesman "come to fix the sink." At other times he arrives after midnight in standard street clothes. His friend has a PO box in a public mail service building and handles Red's incoming and outgoing correspondence. He also provides food and laundry service for which he is paid out of the rebel's earnings as a writer. Red has an exercise machine in his attic quarters as he is aware that health is the key to continuous high-level activity.

When Red leaves his city hideout, he may head for an old boat that is tied up in the backwaters of a fish harbor. He has an interest in this boat and, on occasion, takes it out for a working vacation. He smokes the fish he catches and they become part of his regular diet. For his stays on the boat he uses his lightweight typewriter and the services of a regular post office box registered to another friend. He drops off his mail and picks up incoming mail late at night after the PO closes. With his fisherman's cap, boots and Levi jacket, he is unrecognizable as a highly competent tax rebel hard at work on his next booklet of instructions on how to bamboozle the tax collector.

So far his strategy of never remaining too long at any of his dozen hideouts has proved successful. He knows that if the IRS launches an all-out campaign they may arrest him, but for now, he is happy in his lifestyle of hideout hopping.

INDIAN HEMP GROWER

Ted Barry is one of his names and assuredly not his real one. He has been growing an herb, and the current establishment claims this is a felonious act. His cover is a tree farm and land restoration project in one of the forested counties of the state of (CENSORED). Remote from this facility is a region of rugged canyons and steep hillsides. Here is where Ted has his herbs growing in large redwood tubs. The growing medium is a lightweight, well-fertilized mixture that he has developed. It's no problem to pick up a tub and move it to another location in a few minutes. The entire "farm" can be moved a mile or more, if necessary, in a matter of a few hours.

A former technical writer for a large aerospace company, Ted has maintained his expertise in electronic technology. Thus his security system for his portable farm consists of both infra-red and motion detection. He can tell instantly if there are any animal or human interlopers in or around his crop. Deer are kept at bay because Ted scatters a chemical analog of mountain lion dung around his private farm.

The economics of his project allow generous expenditures for security, communications and other elements of overhead. At four figures per plant, there is enough profit in the 6-month, seedling-to-sale season to allow almost any measure that will ensure success and Ted employs them all.

You might term this herbal farm an ultimate hideout arrangement and so it is. Remote, hidden, camouflaged, well-protected and portable, it fulfills virtually all of the criteria for a secure sanctuary.

Thus, if whatever you do is anathema to others, it would be sensible to investigate what high-tech, high-profit people are doing currently.

NOTE: The morality of legal and illegal drugs is not within the scope of this book. We offer information on hideouts in the West and if a few relate to activities currently unlawful that is incidental.

THE GYPSY

Dave doesn't bother with a last name and, like Zorba the Greek, says, "I got hands and feet, what does it matter what I do?" He travels about in his good-sized camper doing whatever comes to hand, from picking fruit along the Snake River in Idaho to helping run a long tom at a Mother Lode mine site.

Once a well-paid technician in a Pasadena, California, electronics plant, Dave gave it up to live in his station wagon. That was so much fun he used the last of his savings to buy a comfortable pickup camper.

He calls himself a tire tramp and has no schedule whatsoever. Some years he stays north in winter and has been known to spend even a hot summer in the desert as long as he has shade and a source of cool water.

It would be difficult to keep track of Dave. He hasn't bothered with mail for many years and calls on the people he wants to see rather than write letters. Often he will have a new campground for his cook-out meals every night.

Dave is doubtless the modern counterpart of the saddle tramps of the old west who lived on or near their horses for years on end. Like these old cowboys, he works only when the metal "horse" he uses needs feed or overhauling. The rest of the time he enjoys nature on a one-on-one basis.

He observes that he now sees his previous life as one of pure BS. "They want us to work for 45 years and then get a couple of years off for good behavior," he says pointing out that the average social security retiree only lives to collect for a few years despite what is heavily publicized in the press.

Dave is a good example of what might be termed the portable hideout lifestyle. He isn't really hiding from anything or anyone but his nomadic and adventurous mode of living would ensure a high degree of privacy and independence.

The last time I saw Dave was across a campfire in the Nevada desert where he confided that he had learned more from fellow tire tramps than he ever did in college.

BACKWATER BETTY

The surrounding scenery resembles the South Pacific but it's really just the tangled vines and willows of the California Delta that festoon her aging Owens cruiser. We'll call her Backwater Betty to preserve her anonymity. Once a musician with a leading symphony orchestra, she has retired to living aboard a 35-foot boat moored to an old pier extending out from one of the many isolated Delta islands. She has water and electricity by agreement with one of the island's farmers. With her skiff and outboard she can make it to a general store on the mainland in about half an hour or so.

As a hideout, it's almost a classic, but she really doesn't intend to have anyone think of it in that way. While she likes her privacy, she is not averse to an occasional visit by some musically-minded person. She'll play tapes of the great masters and relate interesting stories of the composer's lives. At rare intervals she assembles her English horn and accompanies the music.

I never asked about her source of income nor did she volunteer this information. One must conclude that she has some sort of small pension. Actually, as we've pointed out elsewhere, some hideout living requires minimal funding and her floating home was definitely in this category.

What can you do all day in a setting such as this? Oddly, there are often not enough hours in the day to do all you want! For example, just behind her boat is a colony of raccoons that tumble, fight, screech and play all the time. Just watching them is an entertainment to beat any TV screen. Then there is the chance to take the skiff and go collect wild berries, artichokes or volunteer apples and plums. When that season is over, one can fish or set traps for the billions of crayfish that call the Delta home. Then there is *always* some maintenance work on the boat — painting, polishing, repair. Visitors do drop by at intervals and they must be conversed with and offered coffee and snacks. Then routine shopping, visits to a dentist and all the other mundane tasks that we're all involved in must be accommodated. Yes, for a hideout lifestyle, it can be and is a busy and fulfilling one.

HIDEOUT LOCATION REVIEW

OVERVIEW

Inasmuch as we are limiting our scope to hideouts in the eleven Western states, let's have a look at the region in a general way. Viewed from a satellite, the most significant feature would be the tremendous variety of terrain: coastal plains, high mountains, inland valleys, deserts, river deltas, large lakes. At night another aspect becomes apparent. Where is everybody? Except for the relatively few large cities and scattered towns, most of the land is uninhabited. In fact, somewhere around 90 percent of all Westerners live on less than 10 percent of the land! This is great for all of us hideout advocates. We have plenty of room from which to choose our favorite locations!

Drop down from satellite height to ten thousand feet and fly over certain parts of the West at night and you won't see a single light. Vast reaches of Nevada desert, Idaho wilderness and the Rocky Mountains have not a single resident of any permanence. Oh, you might see a backpacker's campfire on occasion, but most of the time, velvet-black darkness prevails. Lovely.

State boundaries are artificial, so let's examine the West from the standpoint of terrain. Proceeding from west to east here's what we find. Along the Pacific coast there are hills and low mountains interspersed with sloping plains and sand dunes. Inland valleys are often wide bordered by both low and high mountain ranges. As one moves eastward from the Cascades and Sierras, the land turns to a vast desert often separated by north/south mountains. The Nevada region is often thought of as mostly desert but it has a surprising number of discontinuous mountains and more water than you may have attributed to the area. Desert of one type or another (high, low, arid, bountiful) encompasses millions of acres providing a varied selection for that type of hideout. In the same way, extensive mountainous areas such as the Rockies, offer sanctuary to those who prefer more green flora than cactus and chaparral.

Vast parts of the easternmost states begin to roll into the prairies that are so characteristic of the Middle West. These plains are crossed by rivers and interspersed with woods and canyons making them ideal for remote hideout inventory.

To summarize this introduction; be the guest of the West. Select your hideout from one of the world's best inventories.

Following are descriptions of hideout locations that I have visited in the past 20 or 30 years and found to be suitable from most standpoints. The question might be asked — Are you not giving away information that would be of value to potential oppressors? My answer to that would be the same as to the question whether divulging the locations of great hot springs might overcrowd or destroy some of them. Really not, because of the great abundance of hot springs, *and* hideouts. The following data might reveal information that would be harmful to all of us hideout lovers, but I think that the over-all positive effect will outweigh the disadvantages. After all, if I didn't write this book, how would you, the freedom-loving reader, know what I've learned?

In summary, it's a trade-off as we have all found much of life to be.

DESERT

Winters are cold and blustery in the northern latitudes and when the birds start to fly south it's time for hideout lovers to head for places like Death Valley, California, Southern Arizona and New Mexico. I've always enjoyed poking around the side canyons of Death Valley, exploring the old ghost towns, the many abandoned mines and, especially, Furnace Creek to pick up ten pounds of wonderful, fresh, natural dates for just $10. That great food will keep your hideout in vitamins and minerals for many weeks. The ideal hideout enclosure for this region would be a snug trailer or camper. For maxium privacy just pretend to be Mr. Average Tourist with a billed cap reading "ACME FEEDSTORE," a short-sleeved Hawaiian shirt and a garrulous manner. Ladies can carry a big bag stuffed with copies of *Cosmopolitan* and *Harlequin* romance novels. With this disguise, no one of consequence will ever bother you and you can stay in the public campgrounds untroubled.

Alternatively, you can seek out some of the seldon-visited areas, but be sure of having suitable traction for your vehicle. There's a lot of treacherous sand in DV.

GRAND CANYON COUNTRY. *If you are really serious about having a hideout that no one will find, consider this formidable area. No roads, no people and often no water. However, if you have explored regions like this you'll know that there are often hidden canyons with hot and cold springs, cottonwoods and willows, ferns and wildflowers and lots of entertaining life like ground squirrels, chipmunks and cottontails. From my own experience with areas such as this, I know that it is a mind-expanding one. With no interference from alleged civilization, one can tune into the earth, the solar system and, in time, the cosmos itself. When it's just you and these ancient bluffs, the circuit is direct and without resistance, like using gold or silver wires for electronic connections. Hideouts can often produce much more than you expected in terms of enlightenment. But you'll have to try it yourself and alone. Take care on those crumbling edges of mesas and escarpments. Bring water and an open mind.*

A phenomenon of the new American lifestyle on wheels is quite evident in Southern Arizona where thousands of campers and trailers invade the vast open desert regions and take up residence without charge. While there has been some bureaucratic effort to sell permits, most of the tire tramps and hideout lovers I know just boogie on out into their favorite mesquite country, lower the awning, put out the folding chairs and start soaking up all that lovely sunshine.

A smattering of these people gather in enclaves (and there is a big gathering around Quartzsite for rockhounds each year) but the people that I relate to are the loners who like to stake a squatter's claim to their own remote and beautiful stretch of pristine desert land. Don't forget to check out the green and cool Colorado River as it flows with great solemnity below Lake Havasu City and Parker. If you enjoy water with your sand, this is definitely the place to hang out.

One great tipoff that a place is livable is the presence of Indian ruins. These you will find if you get out your New Mexico map and find the little towns of Silver City and Hurley. Just north are the Gila River remnants of an ancient culture and all around this area are flowing hot springs. 'Nuff said.

I can't really leave the subject of the desert without mentioning one of my favorites — the entire state of Nevada. Most people remember it as being quite flat since travel is by high-speed roads that seek out the lower regions. But if you will examine a topographic map you'll find that Nevada has almost continuous mountain ranges separating the vast desert plains. If you explore the Silver State, you'll no doubt discover what many mobile hideout people have. It's lots greener and has more water than you've been led to believe. For example, some of the largest springs in the world are located near Alamo and not far from there, at the head of Meadow Valley wash near Caliente, is a verdant canyon that could be the model for a sand-surrounded Shangri-La. One parting shot on Nevada. It would be easy to write about hideouts even if one were limited geographically to that one state!

MOUNTAINS

Traditionally, those seeking sanctuary have taken to the high country. It happened after the fall of the Roman Empire and it's happening today in troubled places worldwide. Rugged, jagged terrain, heavy tree-growth and plenty of remote canyons make mountainous country ideal for long or short-term privacy and the construction of permanent or semi-permanent facilities.

Oddly, one can often find good locations not far from so-called civilization. I recall finding a plastic shack not ten minutes walk from the Zephyr Cove Inn at south Lake Tahoe. It was occupied by a young couple who were working at the Inn and saving every penny for a land purchase. Had it not been for someone who likes to push through heavy manzanita to see what they can find, it's likely they would have never been discovered at all. Naturally, I kept their little secret and learned that they later settled in a remote area in Maine.

I have the feeling that most people who are seriously into mountain strongholds want to be far from the madding crowd and, thus, here's a review of some that fit this description.

If you want to mix great beauty with your hideout, consider the vast High Sierras that range from Mojave to north of Quincy, California, a distance as the crow flies of more than 300 miles. In this vast complex of high (15,000-foot) peaks, crashing rivers and seldom-traveled trails, you'll find an abundance of locations suitable for almost any kind of hideout you envision. There are dozens of abandoned towns, and mines by the thousands. I recall that I once considered buying an old mine because it was located in such a remote and picturesque location. It was in a canyon containing the clear, sparkling waters of Licking Fork (yes, that was the name!) Creek. Ferns and many lush plants sprang up on the sides of crystal pools that felt so refreshing during the hot summer. Incidentally, I often wondered why they worked so hard at that mine shaft when paradise was theirs for the taking!

This particular mine would have made a great hideout location because of its remoteness and the steep, almost impassable trail that led to it. Not too many miles north was another region with many hideout potentials. This is the terrain containing the headwaters of the Mokelumne River. Three forks, the north, middle and south, make up this great flow and each have an abundance of tributary canyons that are as rugged as the ones the Sierras contain. If I were planning a permanent facility, I would certainly consider this savagely beautiful expanse, even taking into consideration the often chilly winters and heavy snows.

SHERWOOD. One of Robin Hood's secrets of success in evading the Sheriff of Nottingham was that he had all those wonderful trees to hide behind. And it was almost cheating to be wearing green too! Fortunately for all of us hideout lovers, Weyerhauser hasn't cut down all the trees in the Western U.S. In fact, the last time I checked, there seemed to be more trees than ever! It would require another small book to list all the many opportunities that one has to create a totally secure hideout in the dense forests of many of the mountainous states. From Hobbit-type smials under a fallen redwood to treehouses 70-feet up, you have many chances to put your creativity to good use. And there are bonus features such as good air, friendly forest creatures (for the most part), running brooks and the wisdom of the forest. Stay long enough around big trees and they'll communicate some interesting facts about their subtle consciousness and the interconnectedness of all things.

Incidentally, the Sierras have been the sanctuary of those who grow forbidden herbs. Many of these *ad hoc* hemp farmers pack in their seeds and equipment, plant and nurture a crop, harvest and dry it, and then serenely walk out. That's how still, silent and secretive those towering peaks can be. The word would have to be...protective.

An integral part of the Ring of Fire that semi-circles the Pacific Basin are the snow-capped Cascades that originate in Northern California and extend north through Oregon and Washington into British Columbia, Canada. One of the highest peaks is magnificent Mount Shasta, dead center in Northern California just south of the Oregon border. Here are often gathered spiritually-oriented nature lovers who would no doubt be sympathetic to those seeking solace in solitude. Within sight of Shasta are many thick forests that would be appropriate for a variety of hideout dwellings either on a purchase, lease or squatting basis. I will leave it to your discretion as to which would be most suitable.

As you journey northward, towns grow smaller and one finds fewer people. I have often traveled for miles by foot, and even by car, and not seen a single soul in or around the towering Cascades. But if this isn't remote enough for you, then travel eastward to the neighboring state of Idaho. Here in the center of this sparsely populated state you'll find the largest wilderness area in the U.S., the splendid and pristine Selway-Bitterroot Wilderness region. And even with its 1.8 million acres, it's still only a small part of a larger area that is free of roads, people, and McDonalds.

Take a map of Idaho and draw a line connecting the following towns: Stanley, Salmon, Lolo Hot Springs, Grangeville, McCall, Banks and back to Stanley. The area inside the huge oval is mostly uninhabited and with only a few dirt roads and trails. What a great opportunity to find yourself a hideout location to beat any other!

GREAT HIDEOUT COUNTRY. *Get your supplies in Hamilton (lower right) and then disappear for as long as you like in this roadless region!*

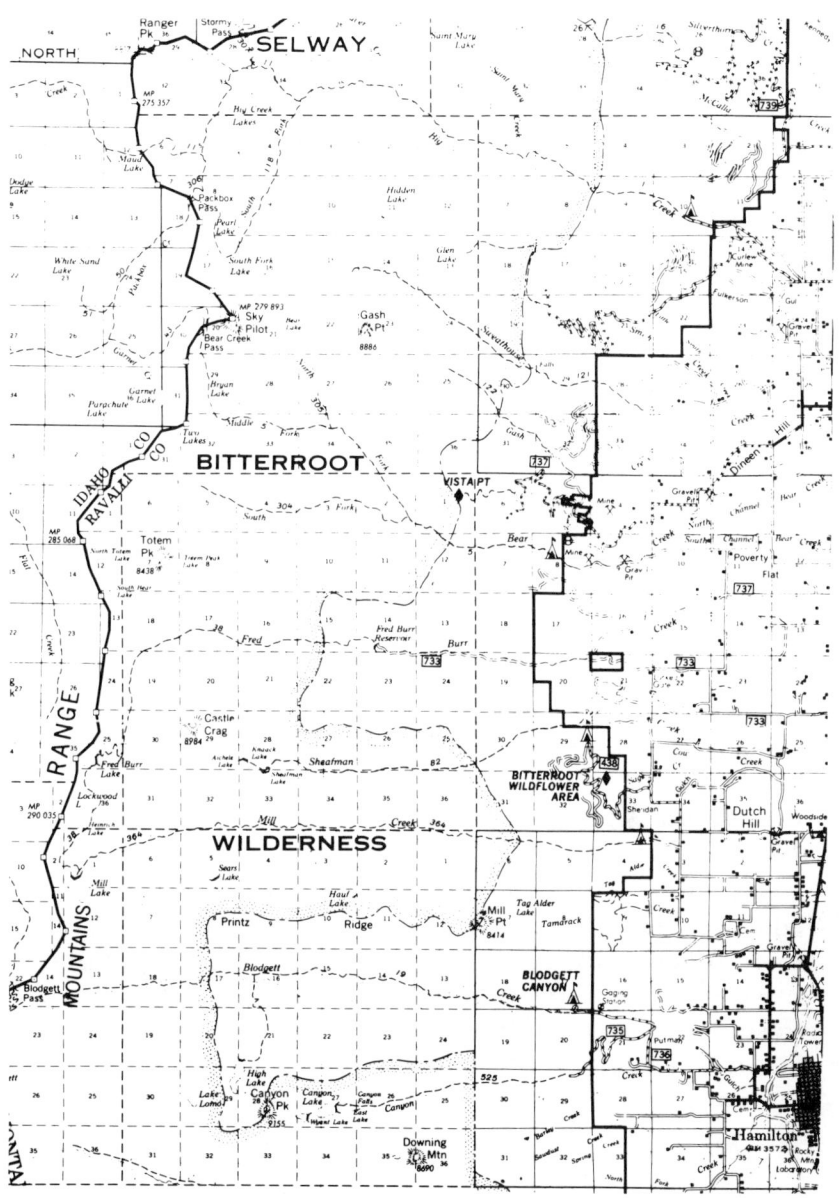

One of the great successes of establishing a base in the wilderness was within the area circumscribed, by a man named Sylvan Hart. Many years ago he trekked into the area east of Burgdorf (near Riggins) and created a Robinson Crusoe "island" on the banks of the South Fork of the Salmon River. Totally on his own he grew his food, shot game, built a blacksmith shop and actually made his own tools and guns! A most remarkable hideout expert, Hart was the subject of a book titled *Last of the Mountain Men* that may be in your local library. I highly recommend it to anyone who plans to make it on their own far from civilization and the local hardware store.

Another plus factor (which we discuss at length elsewhere) is that many of Idaho's nearly 300 hot springs are located within this central core of free living. What could be better than to locate your hideout and have it boast hot running water!

South of well-publicized Sun Valley is the airport town of Hailey. Here you can rent or charter a plane and survey thousands of square miles of wilderness Idaho in a matter of hours. Or, alternatively, drive your RV to one of the jumping off points like Cape Horn or Challis and with your backpack, explore this hidden interior on foot.

Any way that you go will be rewarding in knowledge and closeness to the best of Mother Nature, I personally guarantee it. And one last remark. Don't forget the possibilities of exploring by raft. Idaho is one of the best states for this great sport.

Obviously, we could go on for many pages about mountain hideout resources. The incredible Rocky Mountains that bisect America would require an entire book. But suffice for this summary to say that if you get out your map of the Western U.S., you'll see that there is such an abundance of mountainous terrain that it would require ten lifetimes to see a fraction of it.

UNINHABITED SHORELINES. The road turns in at Rockport and from that point north you have the coast of California just about all to yourself. This is typical of many areas even further north — Vancouver Island and the west coast of British Columbia, for example. I can recall an instance where a man built himself a driftwood hideout along the base of a cliff and no one bothered him for years. At last contact, he was still there! If the sound of waves crashing on the beach and the cry of seagulls turns you on, then this might be a fine location to use available materials and create one of the world's best fantasies, a beachcomber's shack with complete privacy. Personally, I can only take that "karsh, whoosh and hiss" sound just so long and then I need some time inland. But for a while, it's great to live on the edge of such a spectacular achievement in planetary design, the great Pacific.

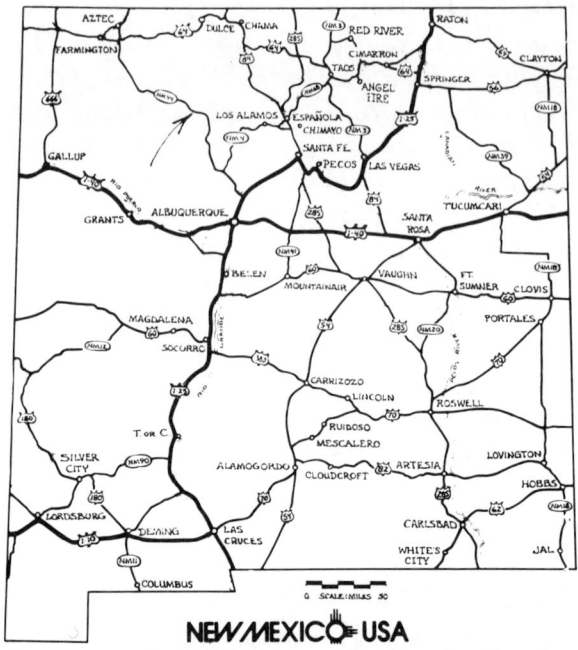

Simplified maps such as this one show only the main roads of a particular area. Thus it is easy to determine the areas of greatest remoteness. It's just common sense that where there are few or no roads, there are few or no people. Fortunately, the off-the-road vehicles now being offered make it easy to reach roadless, hideout locations. And a small plane will make it even faster! Take a look at that region in northwest New Mexico bisected by State Highway 44. Recently I traveled this route rather slowly observing that even the native Indians are very scarce. The region is devoid of any significant development and appears just as it must have 10,000 years ago. Obtain a NM map and check out the area from Cuba to the Blanco Trading Post. You will note that the road crosses the Canon Largo. Although part of the Canon is an Apache Indian Reservation, much of it is public or open land. Also take note of the graded sideroads leading to such remote locales as Pueblo Pintado and Torreon. I will guarantee that even if you don't find the hideout location to suit, you will see some rugged and beautiful terrain unspoiled by hamburger stands and shopping centers.

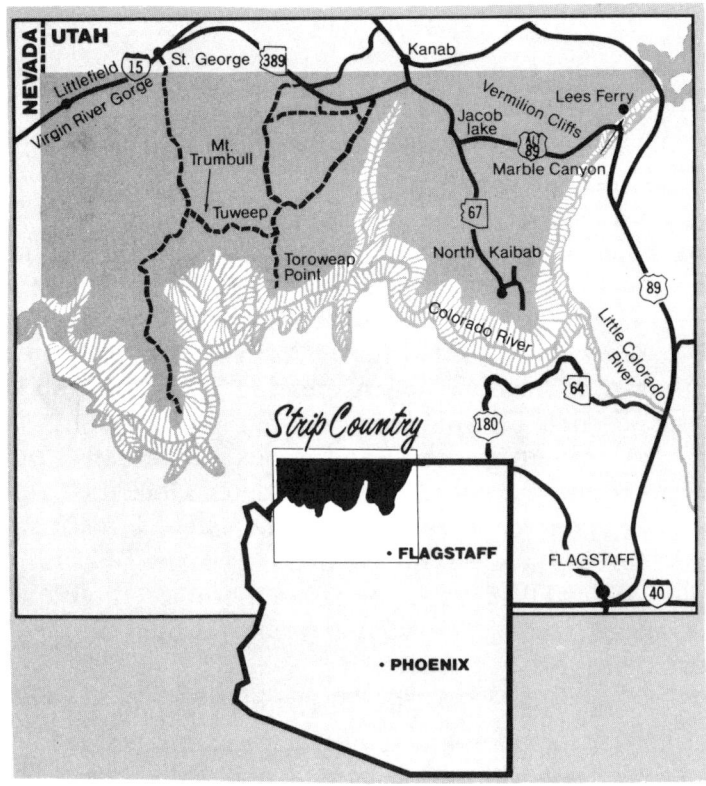

LOOKING FOR THE LONELY PLACES...and finding them. If the island of Manhattan were as sparsely populated as the area shown above, then only 12.4 people would live amidst those towering skyscrapers. Thus, if it's open country you are seeking for your hideout, may I recommend what is known as the Arizona Strip. I was never able to verify the rumor myself, but I understand that in the late '60's, tribes of new age people lived in the roadless and uninhabited canyons that are tributary to the Grand Canyon. Perhaps when you tour this region, you can find out for yourself.

FOUR FAVORITE HIDEOUTS

The Delta

As defined scientifically, a delta is a low plain of alluvial soil interspersed with labyrinthine waterways and exists at the mouth of a river or rivers. Encompassing about 1500 square miles is the California Delta formed by the confluence of the Sacramento and San Joaquin rivers. Here is real Tom Sawyer, Huck Finn country which has really changed little since it was created in its present form after the Gold Rush. It seems that farmers began creating islands by building levees and then pumping out the remaining water. Today there are perhaps a thousand miles of canals, sloughs, backwaters and natural rivers in the delta. Once the haunt of river rats, pirates and people that the establishment would term "dubious," it is STILL the haunt of many free-thinking people. And well it might be since there are thousands of boats, which means that your own boat would be a pebble amidst many other pebbles.

For several years I lived in the Delta aboard an old 75' CG cutter converted to full-time living. It was a life best defined as a moveable feast with people coming and going, lots of fishing and crawdadding, much wild berry picking, swimming around the clock and the major discovery of how to live on about 25¢ a day!

I moved the boat periodically, but NOT ONCE was I boarded by a bureaucrat, except for one year when the tax collection people caught up with me. (They never did that again!)

What I would recommend for the Delta is an older yacht of rather modest appearance. A lot of shiny chrome could attract the light-fingered while you are away hauling up catfish. Move around a bit. After all, it would take ten lifetimes to explore the entire region. If you need an income, there are many ways to have one, including gathering clams for bait, picking berries for market, casual farm labor during harvest season or, if musical, entertaining in the many restaurants and clubs that dot the Delta.

Best time of year is April to November. Winters can be cold and blustery, but still interesting because of all that lovely water!

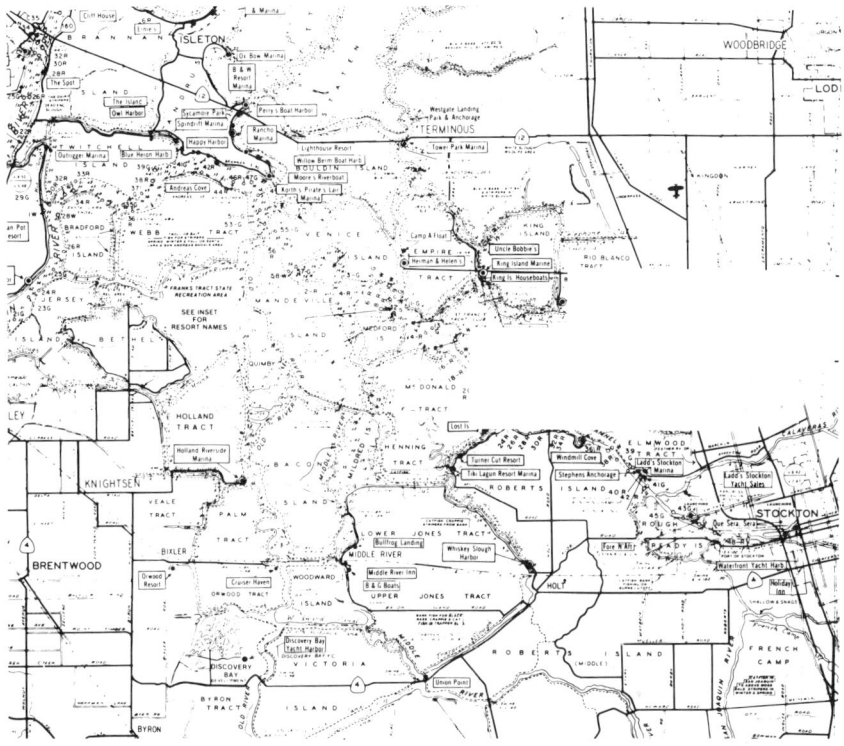

This map shows only a part of the vast Delta region. Actually it extends many miles north and west.

Puget Sound

If you love the ocean, particularly the small-wave kind, islands, greenery and lots of space between you and the next person, then consider the beautiful combination of land and water provided by Puget Sound. To me the entire area is one vast, aquatic hideout just waiting for you to arrive in your boat or RV. You'll have your choice of living on land or the salt water or any combination of the two. What with some 172 islands in the San Juans alone, you will have no problem finding a remote harbor to drop your hook. Also, since many of the islands have no ferry service, once you are settled in you can expect few if any visitors.

Let's take a tour of one of the most beautiful of the San Juans, Orcas Island. It is large enough (57 square miles) to have a variety of scenery yet small enough to have that delightful quality of feeling remote and out of the main stream of alleged civilization. Snug harbors, rolling fields and a surprisingly high peak (Mt. Constitution, 2,409 feet) are but a few of the features of Orcas. There are a few tiny villages on Orcas, Eastsound, Olga, Deer Harbor, but for the most part it is rural and apparently uninhabited. The year 'round population is about 2,200 and most if not all of these people will give what they expect to receive, freedom to live a private life.

Here's a practical suggestion for making an inexpensive and yet scenic tour of the San Juans and Puget Sound. Take the ferry to Orcas Island from Anacortes on the Washington mainland. If you have a car or bike it will be a pleasure to drive or ride to the top of Mt. Constitution. From that fantastic vantage point you can see many of the islands and gain an over-all picture of what you might expect in this hideout heaven. On the return trip, drop in at the Outlook Inn in Eastsound for lunch and a surprise. Just tell them Wild Bill sent you.

A book could easily be written about the potential of Puget Sound as a very private place, but do yourself a favor and go see it in person.

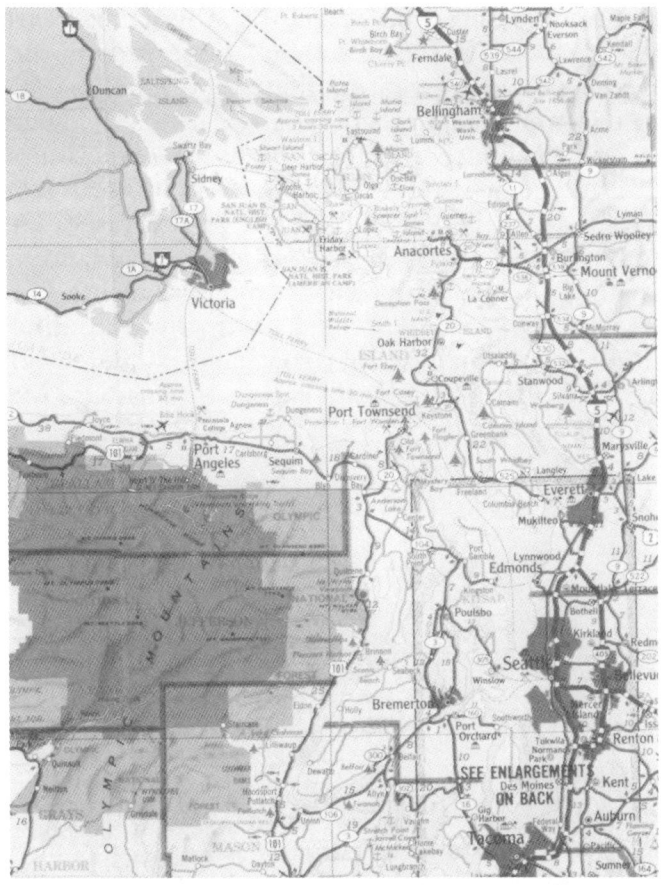

British Columbia

There are so many great hideout opportunities in British Columbia, our friendly Canadian province to the north, that we're including a review as part of the all-inclusive "West." After all, we never intended to limit the discussion to the eleven Western states. BC is certainly an important part of the over-all region.

First, there are almost no hassles in going over the border; I have done it many times with virtually no inspections of consequence. All you need is some proof that you are a U.S. citizen and you can cross and recross as often as you wish.

Furthermore, once you reach the unpopulated areas of British Columbia you'll find yourself alone 99% of the time. And if you go far enough off the roads, you'll enjoy 100% privacy. Here's an example of what we mean. If you drive up the magnificent Fraser River on Highway 1, you'll encounter the little village of Lytton. Take Highway 12 north from this point and you'll still be alongside the great Fraser. The next town is Lillooet, which has a strong resemblance to the pioneer towns of the 19th century...old false fronts, Canadian Indians and tall peaks studded with fir and pine as a backdrop. You'll imagine that you have wandered onto the set of *Rose Marie* or another Royal Canadian Mounted Police melodrama.

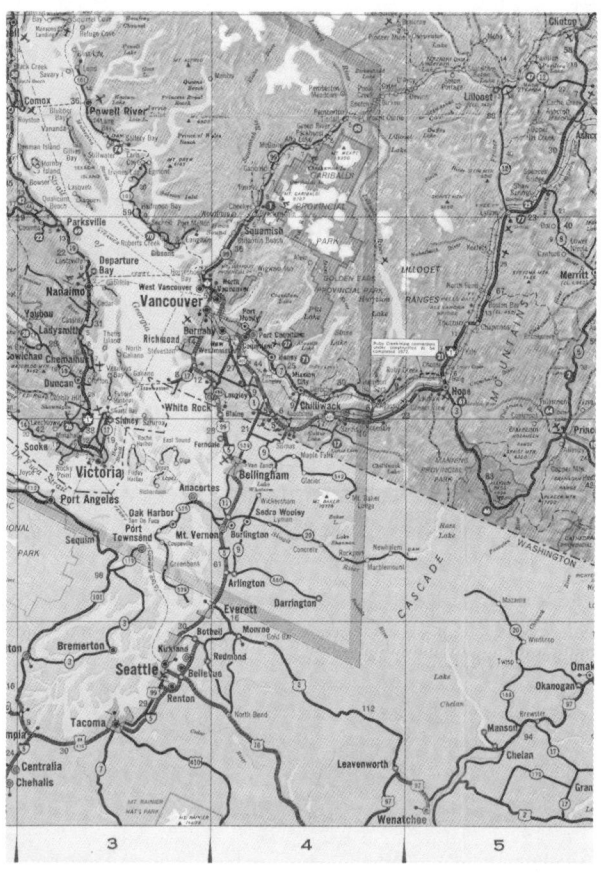

With this frontier town as your base, start exploring in a westerly direction. Paved roads turn to dirt and then these disappear as side trails along tributary rivers and creeks become the only means of exploration. It does not take long for one to experience BC as it appeared 500 or 1,000 years ago. It becomes a true hideout country with possibilities for short- or long-term living in abundance.

Most startling will be your realization that you are examining only one small part of this vast province. Just take a look at the map of BC and you'll see why the opportunities to be your own person in this region are so great! And further, you can continue to explore in a northerly direction towards the Yukon, Alaska and the Arctic Circle. Whenever you feel closed in, drop your projects, jump in your trusty pickup and head for BC. You'll never feel surrounded again.

Nevada

If I had the chance to choose a place and time to live I would select Nevada circa 1850 to 1900. Here was a state with all the freedom that any self-respecting saddle tramp could possibly want. And not only that, but vast deserts with clean air, numerous hot springs, cool rivers, lofty, snow-cloaked peaks and meadows that would have been at home in the Garden of Eden. Fortunately, there haven't been too many changes in much of the Silver State so that those who choose a desert hideout can still indulge their fantasies.

If I had to choose one part of Nevada over another (and this is hard to do when so much of it is intriguing), I would select the southeast corner. Here the resolute explorer can travel for hours on a major road without meeting another car or journey for days on backroads and never see another human being. And if you go far afield, I can almost guarantee that no one will ever hassle you.

Just for fun, travel with me up Highway 93 from the turnoff at I-15 to Highway 375. At first you'll think that the desert sands will never end. But then you'll begin to notice the stark peaks of the Sheep Range westward. If you look closely you may find that rough side road that leads upward into this seldom-explored mountain complex. Here you'll see tracks of cougar and raccoon and the droppings of invisible deer. Springs gush out of rocky outcroppings and form small creeks that eventually disappear into the dry sands below. From the peaks you can see more than a hundred miles in all directions.

One of the areas you will notice, Meadow Valley Wash to the east, appears to be a dry gulch until you explore it by truck, horse or on foot. Then you'll find oases of willow and cottonwood, a small stream that eventually becomes a healthy flow as you approach the upper end of this long and remote arroyo. Only a few ranches dot the landscape and the towns of Carp and Elgin marked on maps turn out to be old railroad stops for water! Turn east from here and you'll find the magic country of Pahranagat Valley with lush meadows, two large lakes and flowing streams that are *warm*. Go see for yourself. It's desert hideout country that will keep you interested indefinitely.

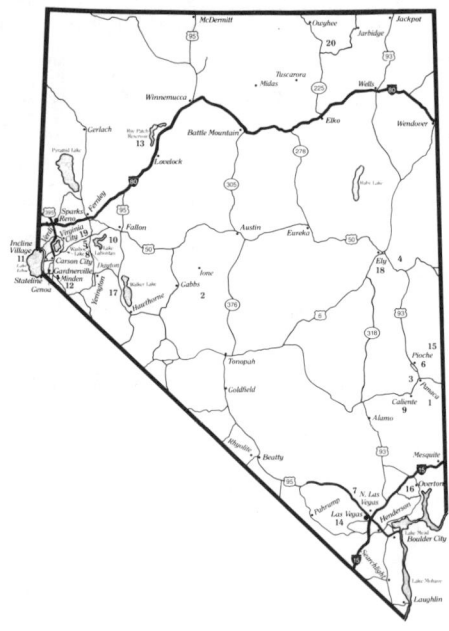

A PHOTO PORTFOLIO OF HIDEOUT FACILITIES

Here, for your review, is an inventory of hideout suggestions. Although only a relatively small sampling, they show the great potential for a private place of your very own. Readers are invited to write the author c/o the publisher for specific hideout facility information, and reader suggestions are most welcome.

What appears to be a storage facility made from an old shipping container is really a small but comfortable apartment with a skylight and ceiling ventilation. Touch a concealed button and part of the wall slides back in "open sesame" fashion. A fine urban hideaway at low cost.

Not only would this former warehouse make a great hideout, it could be used to operate a business — mail order for instance. All you need is a print shop and P.O. nearby.

Oddly, many great hideout locations are located only a few miles from a major metropolis. Here we see the cosmopolitan city of San Francisco across the bay from the

wild hills of Marin County. There are MANY great hideout locations in Marin, including the famous "Gate Five" houseboat enclave.

This quiet and remote waterway is part of the lower Columbia River that separates Washington and Oregon. There are countless opportunities to establish either a floating or landbound hideout in areas where water and land interface.

Change of commercial needs often assigns once bustling waterfront enterprises to derelict status. Here is a restorable small building on pilings on an out-of-the-way bay in southern Washington. Don't restore it to the point where the taxman assesses it.

Supported by giant cedar logs, this floating boathouse would make an ideal hideout. Furthermore, it would not be too difficult to move it with a medium-sized tug.

Painted forest green as camouflage, this mini-hideout has room for a loft bed, two-burner hot plate, a portapotty, closet and small sink. Only 8' x 12' or about 100 square feet, it is adequate as a shelter for one or two dedicated privacy seekers.

Chilean inquisitors could not force me to reveal the location of this "no-permit" hideaway somewhere in the West. Built in segments, each unit has a separate function (bedroom, bath, kitchen and so forth.) Entire hideout is invisible from road below.

Closeup of outdoor patio segment with attached core trailer. The old Fireball 15-footer serves as general purpose kitchen and workroom. (Visible faintly at extreme right.)

The water that ran continuously from that spout was cool and delicious. Odd that it should be so in the midst of this vast Nevada desert region. And even odder when the creek flowing in the foreground came from a stunning blue, almost unearthly crater-like hot spring. That's why the temperature was about 85 F, just right for a good soak. The house was offered to us rent-free. All we had to do was live there and keep vandals from destroying it. There wasn't even any stipulation that we had to fix the roof or paint the kitchen. This type of offer is characteristic of many remote regions where owners of isolated property are grateful for anyone who will act as a caretaker. So if it's a free hideout without

strings that you are seeking, then prowl around some of those Nevada valleys that the tourists to Vegas and Reno never see and probably never will see.

About as isolated as a ranch can be. This one is surrounded by Federal Lands with restricted entry. However, owner has keys to all the gates and year-round access. Privacy plus!

For both living and growing your own, it's hard to beat a quickly-erected shelter of wood and plastic sheeting. As may be noted, this one is barely visible even when the viewer is close up!

Some people make use of forests for their own squatter's shacks. This one could use a leaf pattern painted on its walls.

Not far from a scenic harbor along the Western coast is this abandoned shop. The electricity could be reconnected, the interior refurbished and a comfortable hideout created for minimal expenditures.

Although boarded-up and seemingly abandoned, these three ocean-view homes could probably be restored. You will find many opportunities like this in areas where the departure of a major industry has caused depopulation.

While motorcycling in the vast Los Padres National Forest we discovered this venerable adobe that was probably an early homestead. Often these can be obtained for restoration if privately owned. There is often private land within National Forests.

Although this old warehouse in a down-and-out harbor area appears deserted, there are beautifully-decorated apartments located inside. Stay cool and quiet and you will have no problems creating a great low-cost hideaway almost any place you choose.

Old buildings in economically depressed communities offer many possibilities for development as secure and private hideouts.

Restoration is just a matter of labor and materials. No great secret to making something livable out of an old home or building. And lots cheaper than buying an overpriced condo in some smoggy city!

URBAN HIDEOUTS. *An afternoon spent with a 35mm camera produced the possibilities on this and the next three pages. Here we see an array of houseboats in Sausalito, California.*

TOP: Here we find a place for your boat near a warehouse complex. BOTTOM: A large old steamer that could be purchased by a group of privacy seekers.

Here is an unused pier to which you could tie your boat for free. There are similar possibilities for privacy seekers in many coastal cities.

Some partially hidden trailers and campers. Look around, and you'll find lots of places to park an RV out of the sight of prying eyes.

Partially hidden by productive apple tree, this shop-residence was developed from an old school bus. Land was leased from owner of remote parcel in redwood country. All this and spring water too.

Low-cost addition to an old trailer provides more spacious hideout for single parent and blind son. So remote that building inspectors will never find it.

Author's trailer parked just behind the Sheriff's headquarters in a California coastal city. Note microwave tower to right of trailer. No hassles in a two-week stay proving that fortune does favor the audacious!

If you're buying land, don't forget that the place at the end of the road has the most built-in privacy.

Treehouses can be simple or elaborate depending on your length of stay and personal needs. I have seen them with hot and cold running water plus all the other amenities.

Built to serve as lunch stands, these lonesome shacks could be moved and refurbished as compact living quarters.

Suggest that exteriors be shingled for durability and low-cost. Want a new locale? Then pickup with forklift and move!

Huge mansion was built on remote site sans permit. Most lumber was milled from timber found on land. Water from spring is piped into this spacious hideaway.

Closeup of building above showing simple log and board/batt construction.

ABOVE: Here's the best of several worlds along a rushing creek near Lillooet, BC; a cabin on a mining claim and a source of income (gold, of course!).

ABOVE: A remote and apparently abandoned miner's cabin far from civilization in British Columbia.

ABOVE: Many lumber camps have been abandoned as this one has in southern Oregon. Check with the owners for possible lease or purchase.

Rough, rugged and dry, this almost forbidding landscape is part of the Los Padres National Forest, a million-acre-plus region of California that extends from the Santa Barbara area north to San Luis Obispo. On first inspection one would hesitate to establish a hideout in this seemingly inhospitable terrain. But let's take a closer look.

Below those rocky bluffs is an all-year swimming pool nearly seven feet deep. Here you can bathe and sun and enjoy the peace and solitude that we all need at regular intervals. A perfect place for a casual hideaway adventure!

Hideout structures can be as compact as these "Microhouses" developed by the Holy Terra Congregation Shelter Taskforce. The above photo shows one built of garage doors.

Below is the clerestory-windowed shed that can be built by two men in about 12 hours. In the bottom photo is the "playhouse." Plans for all from Holy Terra c/o the publisher. Interiors are similar to small travel trailers and can be built to suit.

A GREAT HIDEOUT SHELTER. Unless exact directions and a map were provided it is probable that you would never find the "pine pyramid" below. One of my personal favorites as a hideout shelter, I consider it great because it can be built for so little money by anyone handy with a hammer and saw. Four pine logs form the basic structure with hand-split shingles as the combination roof and exterior walls. The only addition that I would make is to spray it in a green-brown leaf pattern so that you would have to bump into it to see it.

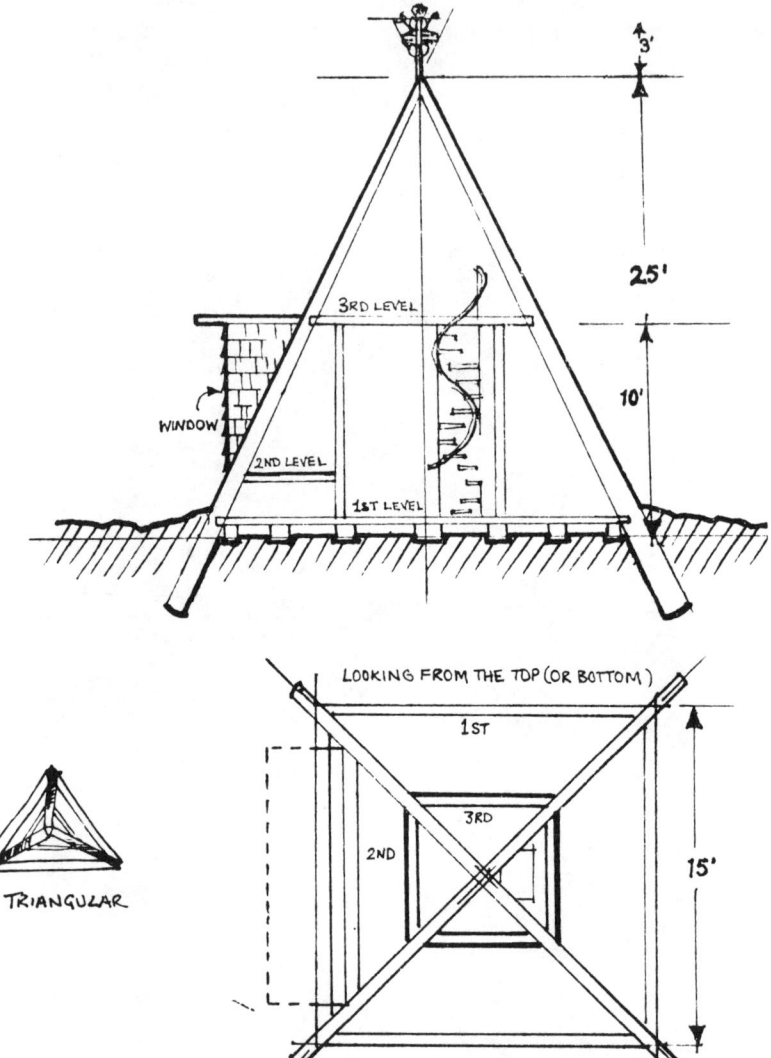

It is estimated that about 3 million Americans live on wheels full time. This number is increasing rapidly as more and more people opt for the gypsy life rather than be stuck in one place with a high mortgage or rent payment. Fortuitously, there are hundreds of new products that make life on the road as pleasant or more so than living in one spot. No one need "rough it" when for much less than a house one can enjoy all the comforts.

Photos courtesy Lancer Campers, Pacoima, CA 91331.

30 Amp Cord 110V Service. (Optional on Models 1000 and 200.) Secure, compartmentalized locking storage for 30 amp 110V cord and 15 amp adaptor.

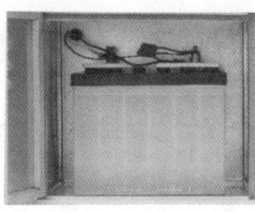

Battery Compartment/Charger. (Optional on Models 1000 and 200.) Locking battery storage offers 12V power on or off the truck.

Fingertip Latches and Plastic Trim on Openings. Out-of-the-way fingertip latches hold tight and look great. Finished plastic trim on opening insures no snags or splinters.

Visual LPG Gauge. (Optional on Models 1000 and 200.) Maintains accurate LPG storage. Automatic pressure check valve integrated into system. 5-gallon capacity each.

Large Wheel Well Access. Ample storage area for tools, barbecues or portable generators. Door sealed to the outside.

hydro flame **Furnace.** 16,000 BTU fully automatic forced-air furnace. Maximum efficiency with wallmounted temperature control. (Optional models 1000 and 200)

Stereo Ready. All units pre-wired 12V for optional stereo unit, plus pre-wiring for optional speakers and antenna. (Optional on models 1000 and 200)

Tinted Radius Sliding Windows. Non-protruding with safety glass and sliding screens. (Solar Reflective Optional)

Dual Holding Tank w/Tow Bar Specially designed holding tanks allow for truck bumper clearance. Optional steel tow bar makes towing safe and secure. Class 1 rated.

Systems Monitor Panel (Self-contained models only). Instant information at a glance shows battery condition, level of fresh water and holding tanks

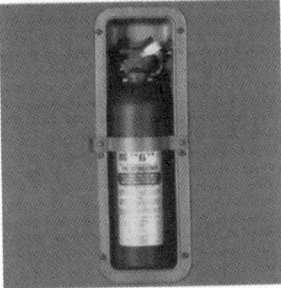

Recessed Fire Extinguisher. Recessed to keep out of the way, yet easy to reach for emergencies. 2-lb. capacity.

Locking Water Fill Door. Handy inlet with screw cap is easy to fill, protects your fresh water supply.

No need to sacrifice comfort when your hideout has wheels, as you can plainly see by this abundance of features, both standard and optional.

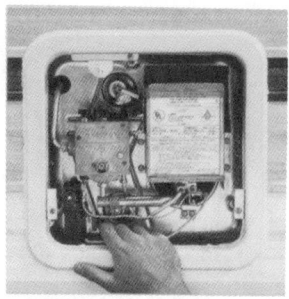

Water Heater. (Optional on Models 1000 and 200.) Upgraded all the way! Electric ignition and auto-relight feature. Flushmount radius door design. 6-gallon capacity.

Deadbolt Latch and Assist Bar. Lighted entry handle with switch inside. Flushmounted, durable door handle. Keyed deadbolt lock for extra protection.

12-Volt Connector - Bumpers - Camper Guides. Molded connector makes hook-up simple. Bumpers afford thorough protection. Camper guides make line-up easy.

Air Conditioning or 12-Volt Cooler. (Optional; wiring standard on s/c models) For that extra measure of comfort. Cooler plumbing only also available as option.

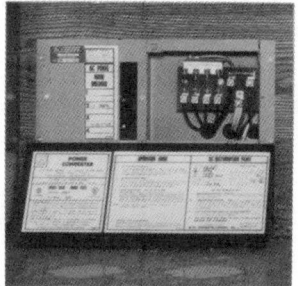

Power Center (Optional on Models 1000 and 200. A centralized 32 amp electrical panel for easy access and maximum space utilization.
Automatic Battery Charger.

98

Large delivery truck provides lots of room for mobile hideout resident. Note sturdy framework which permits carrying everything you need to be independent. Frame would also provide support for camouflage netting in forest setting.

Legal place to park was negotiated by the owner of this pickup camper. In time, those trees and shrubs could hide the rig. Although low profile, there's still room for holiday merriment — note the Christmas tree lights!

Even more privacy was obtained by owner of this small trailer. It is completely surrounded by high fence and with locked gate. Hideout status is assured. Located in high-rent district of coastal resort city.

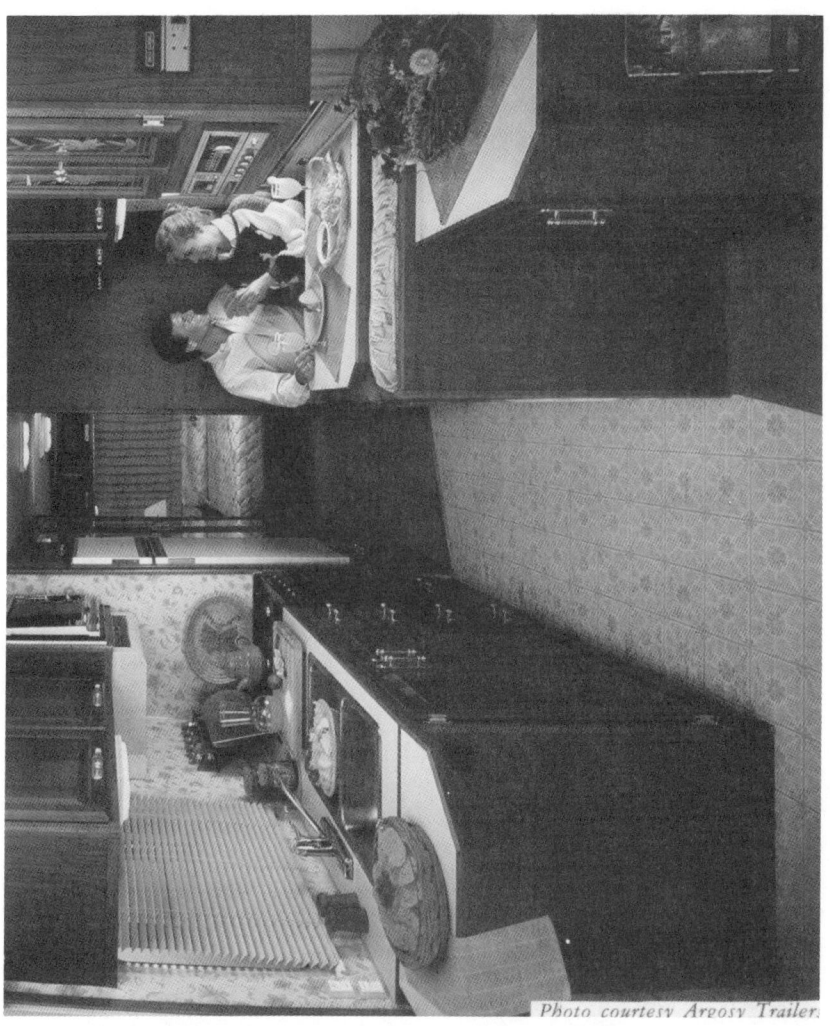

Photo courtesy Argosy Trailers

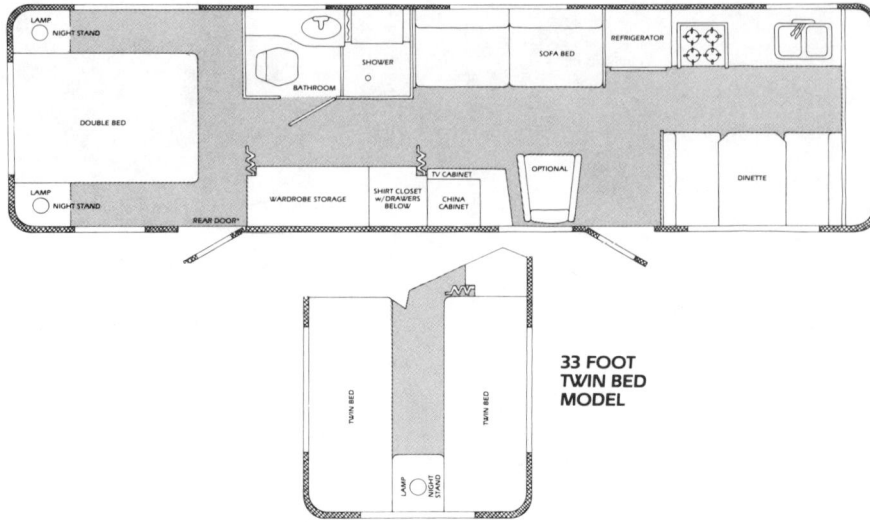

To me, the modern travel trailer is the ultimate mobile hideout. On Page 101 we see a compact kitchen, dinette, and a small but comfortable bedroom. Not shown, a bath and shower and living area. Who really needs more? Above are some typical floor plans. So when you are considering establishing a hideout in ANY area, take the time to check out some of the new trailers.

Specifications

SPECIFICATIONS
```
GVWR ....................... 8,300#
GAWR ....................... 8,000#
Factory Dry Weight............... 6235#
Additional Allowable Weight ...... 2065#
    (Including options, personal cargo & fluids)
Hitch Weight..................... 685#
Overall Length.................... 399"
Exterior Height .................. 108"
Exterior Height w/Air............. 116"
Exterior Width.................... 96"
Interior Height................... 6'7"
Fresh Water Tank w/Drain ........ 50 Gal.
Black Water Tank ............... 30 Gal.
Grey Water Tank................. 35 Gal.
```

Standard features

CHASSIS
    Dura Torque Axles (2) 4;000#
    12" Electric Brakes — All Wheels
    Wheels, Styled, Painted, W/Hub Covers
    Manual Hitch Jack

EXTERIOR
    Horizontal LP Compartment W/Cover
    Awning Rail, Curb-Side Patio
    Front Window Rock Guard Awning
    Exterior Lockable Storage Compartment
        (Above Floor Line)
    4 Roof Vents (2 Powered)
    Storage Compartment, Sewer Hose & Power Cord

WINDOWS & DOOR
    Entry Door W/Window & Keyed Deadbolt
    Screen Door
    Windows, Tinted, Jalousie
    Escape Window, Bedroom, Roadside
        (N/A, Double Door Units)

Here are quite a number of reasons why I think that a great hideout can be manifested in a compact, easily towed trailer. New or used, they offer more living comfort than many houses and apartments. And best of all, you can change the view from your picture window anytime you choose.

STANDARD FEATURES CONT'D.

DECOR INTERIOR
  Mini-Blinds, All Windows
    (Excluding Front,
    & door(s))
  Side Close-Out drapes,
    Living, Dining,
    and Bedroom
  Full Width, Rear Drapes,
    Front & Rear Windows
  Pull Shade, Entry Door(s)

DECOR BEDROOM
  Twin or Full Bed
  Innerspring Mattress(s)
  Full Width, Rear, Overhead Cabinet
    (With Hardwood Doors)
  54" Wardrobe, W/Mirrored Doors
  Shirt Closet w/Drawers

DECOR EAT-IN KITCHEN AREA
  Spice Rack
  Hardwood Cutting Board (Sink Cover)
  Convertible Dinette

DECOR LIVING ROOM
  China Cabinet, W/Glass Doors, With
    TV Cabinet Below
  Sofa-Bed

APPLIANCES
  Furnace 35,000 BTU, W/Elect. Ignition
  4-Burner Range-Oven (W/Glass Door and Light)
  Range Exhaust Vent, W/Fan & Light
  RM2600 Series Refrigerator 2-Way
  6 Gallon Water Heater W/Pilot
  Smoke Detector
  Fire Extinguisher (5BC)

ELECTRICAL
  Exterior, Lighting Package, Includes Lights
    For: LP Service, RS Utility, and Patio
  Exterior 120 Volt Outlet
  Systems Monitoring Panel
  GFI Protection (Bath & Exterior Outlets)
  "Pre-Wire" For Radio
    (Incl. 4 Wired Speakers and Antenna)
  "Pre-Wire" For Air Conditioning
  Brass Table Lamp(s) (120 Volt Lamps)

SYSTEMS-LPG-WATER-WASTE
  30 lb. Steel LPG Bottles
  LPG 2-Stage Regulator, W/Auto,
    Change-Over
  Lockable Water Fill
  City Water Fill W/Regulator

Optional features

CHASSIS
  Spare Tire & Wheel
  Spare Tire Winch
  Power Hitch Jack
  (4) Retractable Balancing Jacks (W/Handle)

EXTERIOR
  Awning, Curbside Patio
  Awning, Center Support
  Rear Rockguard

WINDOWS & DOORS
  Bedroom Entry Door W/Window,
    Screen Door, W/Keyed Deadbolt, Dbl. Step,
    & Assist Handle
  Safety Glass Windows

DECOR INTERIOR
  Sherbet Color Scheme
  Rosette Color Scheme
  Full Carpet
  Swivel Chair

DECOR BEDROOM
  Bedspreads & Pillows

APPLIANCES
  13,500 BTU Air Conditioner (W/Heat Strip)
  Bi-Fold Range Cover
  Micro-Wave W/Priority Switch
  6 Gallon Water Heater W/Elect. Ignition
  RM2800 Series Refrigerator 2-Way
  Gas Detector

ENTERTAINMENT & SOUND SYSTEM
  AM/FM/Cassette Stereo, Located In
    China Cabinet
  TV Ready: Includes TV Antenna, 2 Outlets,
    Complete Cable Service Prep., & Rear
    TV Bracket (In Bedroom, Shipped Loose)

ELECTRICAL
  2nd Battery Deep Cycle

SYSTEMS-LPG
  40 lb. Steel LPG Bottles

Technical data and photos courtesy Argosy Trailers.

FLOATING HIDEOUTS

Once, in a novel about tax rebels and their battle with the IRS, I had the good guys living aboard an old dredge in the California Delta region. With windows blacked-out, a speedboat for transportation and a fine, jungle-like, backwater location, it was the ultimate waterborne hideout. Best of all, this fictional concept has its real-life counterparts.

Take a look at the map of the 11 Western states and note how much protected water there is. San Diego, San Pedro and San Francisco harbors have many little-used or noticed backwater regions where a hideout boat could be easily and unobtrusively moored. Just east of San Francisco is the vast and virtually unused Delta region mentioned above. This is a 30 x 50 *mile* labyrinth of canals, sloughs, rivers and bays that defy any description. You have to see it for yourself.

The under-populated Oregon coast has harbors where you could live unnoticed for years. Bandon, Coos Bay, Reedsport and Newport are typical. Along central Washington's coast is the great inlet of Gray's Harbor as well as Willpa Bay a few miles south. Then we get into the big time, Puget Sound and the southern reaches of Georgia Strait that opens into Canadian waters. Here are hundreds of islands with thousands of comfortable and safe harbors that are available to boats year-round for free.

Leaving salt water and proceeding inland we find another abundance of seldom patrolled water. The mighty Columbia River has a myriad of sleepy backwaters and ghost towns where even the most far-out stranger and his watercraft would be greeted by yawns. The same is true for the Sacramento River from its origin near Shasta Lake to its final exit into San Pablo Bay. I've spent many years exploring only a fraction of the Sacto's possibilities.

Then there are the lakes, natural and man-made. Take Mead for instance, the giant fresh-water lake created by Hoover Dam. Rent a boat there and you'll soon find a half-dozen delightful bays where you can barbecue all the fish you caught with free driftwood on a beach of pristine privacy. The same waterway hideouts can be obtained on even-larger Lake Powell.

For a summer of exquisite scenery and few interruptions, I'd choose Lake Tahoe. Keep a low profile, don't throw any trash overboard and it's unlikely that anyone will even give you the time of day. Ranging far north you'll find the Yellowtail Reservoir that is so large it exists in both Wyoming *and* Montana. Gigantic Fort Peck reservoir contains the headwaters of the tremendous Missouri River and has enough coastline to accommodate several small European countries. If sunshine every day is your predeliction, then examine the Elephant Butte reservoir which lies in the SE corner of warm and friendly New Mexico.

Just think, I haven't even mentioned such treasures as Flathead Lake in Montana or nearby Coeur D'Alene, both of which are so lovely as to make a word description as futile as it would be inadequate. Obviously, there is no lack of possibilities if a floating hideout is your choice.

WHY A FLOATING HIDEOUT IS A GOOD CHOICE

First of all, the real estate (the land beneath the water that floats your vessel) is free. Waterways are, for the most part, public property based on the ancient agreement of Freedom of the Seas. Part of this liberal view extends to the craft and people who are on the water. It is far less likely that you'll ever be bothered on a boat than if you were in your car or RV. There are fewer people out there and those that are hesitate to violate the sanctity of a floating sanctuary. Even the Coast Guard hesitates to come aboard without an invitation. Furthermore, there is abundant opportunity to appear as though you really belong on the water. Buy yourself an old fishing boat and you have a passport to almost unlimited freedom. All you need do is avoid attracting attention, and this list of no-no's is a good one to post on your compass box.

(1) Don't have anything illegal on board.

(2) Have a good reason for being where you are.

(3) Do nothing suspicious. For example, don't run without lights.

(4) Obey all maritime regulations.

(5) Ensure that your vessel appears totally ordinary at all times.

AN INVENTORY OF FLOATING HIDEOUT OPPORTUNITIES

Small *can* be beautiful when you consider how many small boats now have the comfort features of their much-larger counterparts. A trailerable power or sail boat in the 20-to-25-foot range can easily accommodate from one to four compatible outasiters. Keep in mind that often you will be using the boat only for sleeping. You can cook out on the beach and spend most of your time exploring or doing whatever you choose in, on or under the water. I've always believed that Water Rat was right when he declared in *Wind in the Willows*:

"Nice? It's the only thing. Believe me my young friend, there is nothing, absolutely nothing half so much worth doing as simply messing about in boats. Simply messing — about — in boats."

Incidentally, this book, by Kenneth Grahame, is a storehouse of rollicking stories about living the free life. Ostensibly for children, it obviously contains much valuable advice for so-called grown-ups.

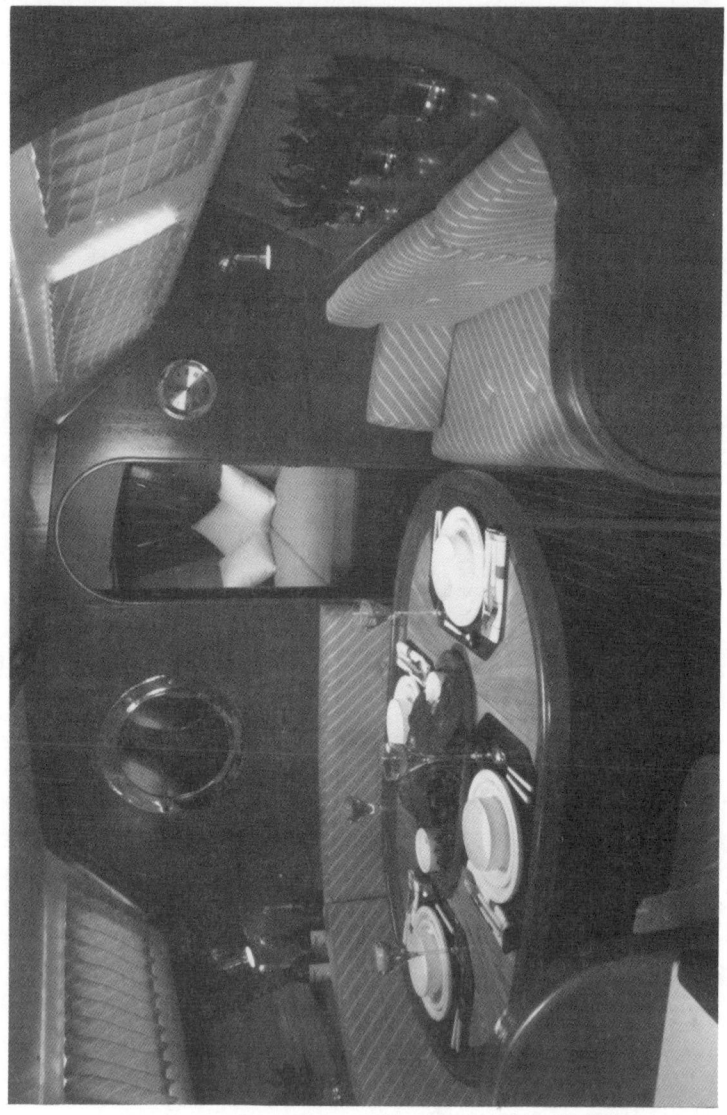

This salon is aboard a 32-foot Freedom sailboat. You can be as comfortable afloat as ashore and enjoy a waterborne hideaway.

The exterior of the sailboat shown on the previous page, again a Freedom boat with many new and unique features that set it apart from other sailboats. For example, the mast has no stays. If you can afford this type of boat you'll have a lifetime hideaway that can take you in comfort to almost any part of the globe.

68' BALTIC TRADER GAFF-RIGGED KETCH
L.O.A.: 68' L.O.D.: 53' BEAM: 15' DRAFT: 7'6"

Powerful Ferro construction built in 1980 to Norwegian Veritas and Royal Danish Ships Inspection for round-the-world sailing. Beautiful, bright and spacious interior with comfortable accommodations for 8-11 people. Equipment includes: 11 sails, Ford 105 h.p. diesel, refrigerator/freezer and much more....This well-proven traditional ocean-crossing vessel is in impeccable order....Must see to fully appreciate....Available for inspection in Fort Lauderdale...Recently reduced to asking only.........

$72,500.00
CALL (305) 463-7765

Big and roomy, this old-style small ship can provide all the comforts plus deep-sea capability. I see it cruising off the coast just for kicks and then wintering on southern waters.

**OWN YOUR OWN ISLAND
CABIN & ACRES OF PRIVACY**

No. 256— 100 acres, $750,000. This untouched island is just the place for the privacy seeker or the ambitious developer. Approximately 100 mostly level acres with ground cover of evergreen trees. 7 protected coves on the waterfront for many hours of oceanfront enjoyment. Reportedly some of the best crab ground in the Puget Sound area. Close to wildlife refuge, marinas and state parks. Mild climate typifies the lower San Juan Island chain. 330-sq. ft. primitive cabin for shelter. Ideal for corporate retreat, resort or private hideaway— $750,000. *Shelton, Wash.*

A perfect match for a boat or fleet would be this ultimate land/water hideout in the Washington area.

FOR SALE
BANK REPO'S AS IS WHERE IS

50' x 16' x 6½' V-12-71 GM, Twin Disc 4.5:1
PRICE **$28,500.00**

55' x 17' x 6½' Twin 6-71 GMs Twin Disc Gears 3:1
PRICE **$26,500.00**

38' x 15' x 6' V8-71 GM, Allison 4.5:1, Flanking Rudders
PRICE **$22,500.00**

ALL VESSELS LOCATED AT ORANGE, TEXAS.

MARINE TOWING CO.

P.O. Box 1700, Bridge City, Texas 77611

(409) 886-4493

82' x 19' x 10' DUTCH BUILT, B&W ALPHA H.D. DIESEL - All completely refitted - All new electric system. 7 K.W. Lister and electronics. Completely sandblasted in & out, Epoxy coated. C.P. propeller, clutch, W.H. control. Sea ready. Owner: P.O. Box 282, Brentwood Bay, B.C., Canada V0S1A0

★ **DREDGES FOR SALE**

'84 MC-915 MUD CAT — 1600 Hrs. 3000' 8"x20' poly pipe with Gheen couplings. All harnessing, pipe trailer + dredge trailers, 8x40 3+4 axel. Extra parts. $120,000. 916-583-3500. 7sept1

10" AMMCO HYDRAULIC DREDGE — 3,000 LF 12" poly pipe (new). Rebuilt 12-71, 3-71, pump, spud cylinders, etc. Excellent mechanical condition. $85,000.00. Call (703) 273-1790. 4aug1

97' CONVERTED MINESWEEPER, 1943, single Enterprise DMR6 diesel, 400 HP @ 400 rpm, 7000 gallons fuel, 2650 gallons water, two generators. 60 KW & 7.5 KW. Located Tortola BVI. **$39,000.** Must Sell! Must Sacrifice! 305/467-3628

An assortment of workboats from a recent issue of Boats and Harbors, *a publication that features this type of vessel. (Send*

$1 for sample copy to Boats and Harbors, Crossville, TN 38555.) Note the low prices (39K for a 97-foot vessel!) which make work boats a great bargain for the dedicated hideout lover. Also, you show a lower profile on a workboat.

61' WOOD HULL TUGBOAT — V-12 Cat, just rebuilt year ago. Generator and all electronics in good condition. Boat needs some cosmetic work done. Easy conversion to shrimper or fishing vessel or leave as work boat. Price **$40,000.** (Neg.). **(904) 234-5378.**

★ **TANKERS FOR SALE**

130' x 20' x 8.5', 100,000 U.S. Gal. TANKER, 222.24 gross tons, built 1931 - Twin 6-71 Detroit Diesel with 5 to 1 reduction, Canadian Registry. Condition fair. $80,000.00 U.S. Harry Gamble Shipyard, Port Dover, Ontario. NOA 1NO. (519) 583-2111. 5jul2

45' WOOD HULL FISHING VESSEL 6-71 Detroit Diesel, hyd. clutch - Walk-around cabin. 1 Head, Si-Tex fath. 55-ch VHF. Currently fishing - Would make good shrimper. **$16,000.00** **(904) 478-8692**

★ **SHIPS FOR SALE**

214' x 32' x 12', 1,000 TON CARGO SHIP, 496 gross tons, built in 1957, 1,000 hsp. Deutz Diesel, Panamanian Registry. Condition good. Price reduced to $100,000.00 U.S. Harry Gamble Shipyard, Port Dover, Ontario. NOA 1NO. (519) 583-2111.   5jul2

SEIZED VESSEL TO BE SOLD AT PUBLIC AUCTION TO THE HIGHEST BIDDER WITH NO RESERVE ON JULY 12, 1986 11:00 AM

57' YACHT

Inspection will be day of sale 8:00 A.M. 'till sale time. Location: Slip 25, Clearwater Municipal Marina, Causeway Blvd., Clearwater, FL

Make: Terre Bonne Marine. Model: Trawler. Year: 1975. Length: 57 feet. Name: "Constellation". Reg. No. (U.S.) 563853. Hull No. Unknown. Present Location: Clearwater Municipal Marina, 25 Causeway Blvd. Clearwater, FL.

For information contact: Col. Al Davenport, Auctioneer

(813) 585-1106

CONFISCATED

Single source of **NATIONWIDE** auction info... GSA, Customs, Marshal, DEA, IRS, bankruptcy & liquidation sales. **UPDATED DAILY** & mailed 1st class **every 2 weeks**. We give you item description, time, place & phone numbers. WE do the work, you reap the benefits!!! Get in the act!!! **BUY** boats, freighters, planes, vehicles, all at **BARGAIN** prices.
DON'T MISS THESE OPPORTUNITIES!!!
6 mos. $29   1yr. $49   INFO PACK $7.50
Order 1 yr. & receive INFO PACK FREE
has auction pointers & procedures & includes more than 1600 successful bids.
SATISFACTION GUARANTEED - ACT NOW!!!
CALL TOLL FREE (800) 327-2049
FL (800) 223-3291
VISA/MC/AmEx or mail check to:
National Auction Bulletin
230H Basin Drive - Ft. Lauderdale, FL 33308
(FL res add 5% sales tax)
OUR 4th YEAR of HAPPY BUYERS

People who use boats in smuggling operations risk losing them when they are busted. That's why there are quite a number of boats coming up for auction or bid regularly. This can be your opportunity to obtain a floating hideout for much less than you would pay regularly. Watch for announcements in your area or write to the address given on the next page. An important precaution — boats seized by the government are often left to languish in some back harbor for months or even years before the endless paperwork is completed. Thus, check the boat out carefully before you buy, since it could be beyond restoration.

WANT A LOW COST BOAT? Write to the Director, U.S. CUSTOMS SERVICE at the address nearest your point of pickup. Or, to get an overview, write to Northrup Worldwide Services, U.S. CUSTOMS SERVICE SUPPORT DIVISION, PO Box 1167, Lawton, OK 73502-1167.

Pac.	Anchorage, Alaska 99501 / 620 E. Tenth Ave., Suite 101	(907) 271-4043	Daniel C. Holland
N.E.	Baltimore, Maryland 21202 40 S. Gay St.	(301) 962-2666	A. Robert Beukirch
N.E.	Boston, Massachusetts 02109 2 India St.	(617) 223-6598	John V. Linde
N.E.	Buffalo, New York 14202 111 W. Huron St.	(716) 846-4374	Carlton L. Brainard
S.E.	Charleston, South Carolina 29402 200 E. Bay St.	(803) 724-4312	Vacant
S.E.	Charlotte Amalie, St. Thomas-Virgin Islands 00801 Main P.O. Sugar Estate	(809) 774-2530	Vacant
N.Cen.	Chicago, Illinois 60607 610 S. Canal St.	(312) 353-6100	Richard Roster
N.Cen.	Cleveland, Ohio 44114 / 55 Erieview Plaza	(216) 522-4284	John F. Nelson
S.W.	Dallas-Fort Worth, Texas 75261 700 Parkway Plaza, P.O. Box 61050	(214) 574-2170	David Greenleaf
N.Cen.	Detroit, Michigan 48226 477 Michigan Ave.	(313) 226-3177	William L. Morandini
N.Cen.	Duluth, Minnesota 55802 / 515 W. First St., 209 Fed. Bldg.	(218) 727-6692	William Knobleuch
S.W.	El Paso, Texas 79985 / Bldg. B, Room 134 Bridge of the Americas P.O. Box 9516	(915) 541-7435	Manny Najera
N.Cen.	Great Falls, Montana 59401 / 600 Central Plaza, Suite 200	(406) 453-7631	Don W. Myhra
Pac.	Honolulu, Hawaii 96806 / 335 Merchant St., P.O. Box 1641	(808) 546-3115	George Roberts
S.W.	Houston/Galveston, Texas 77052 701 San Jacinto St., P.O. Box 52790	(713) 226-2334	Walter D. Sherman
S.W.	Laredo, Texas 78041-3130 Mann Rd. & Santa Maria P.O. Box 3130	(512) 723-2956	Joseph Castellano
Pac.	Los Angeles/Long Beach, California / 300 S. Ferry St., Terminal Island 90731	(213) 548-2441	Alice M. Rigdon
S.E.	Miami, Florida 33131 77 S.E. 5th St.	(305) 350-4101	Harry W. Carnes
N.Cen.	Wilwaukee, Wisconsin 53202 517 E. Wisconsin Ave.	(414) 291-3924	Clinton P. Littlefield
N.Cen.	Minneapolis, Minnesota 55401 110 S. Fourth St.	(612) 787-3990	Robert W. Nordness
S.Cen.	Mobile, Alabama 36601 250 N. Water St.	(205) 690-2106	Harvey Perry
S.Cen.	New Orleans, Louisiana 70130 423 Canal St.	(504) 589-6353	Joel R. Mish
N.Y.	New York, New York New York Seaport Area, New York, New York 10048 Customhouse, 6 World Trade Center	(212) 466-5817	John J. Martuge
	Kennedy Airport Area, Jamaica, New York 11430 Cargo Bldg. 80, Room 2E	(718) 917-1542	Sam Banks
	Newark Area, Newark, New Jersey 07114 Airport International Plaza	(201) 645-3760	Max G. Willis
S.W.	Nogales, Arizona 85621 / International & Terrace Sts., P.O. Box 670	(602) 287-9163	Peter F. Gonzalez
S.E.	Norfolk, Virginia 23510 / 101 E. Main St.	(804) 441-6546	Phil Spayd
N.E.	Ogdensburg, New York, 13669 / 127 N. Water St.	(315) 393-0660	W. Richard Nystrom
N.Cen.	Pembina, North Dakota 58271 / Post Office Bldg.	(701) 825-6201	Raymond J. Hagerty, Jr.
N.E.	Philadelphia, Pennsylvania 19106 2nd & Chestnut Sts.	(215) 597-4605	Anthony Piazza
S.W.	Port Arthur, Texas 77642 / 4550 75th St.	(409) 724-0087	Richard J. Garcia
N.E.	Portland, Maine 04112 / 312 Fore St., P.O. Box 4688	(207) 780-3326	Emery W. Ingalls
Pac.	Portland, Oregon 97209 / 511 N.W. Broadway	(503) 221-2865	Clyde Kellay, Jr.
N.E.	Providence, Rhode Island 02903 / 24 Weybosset St.	(401) 528-5081	Joseph Kenny
N.E.	St. Albans, Vermont 05478 Main & Stebbins St., P.O. Box 111	(802) 524-6572/8	Frank R. Spendley
N.Cen.	St. Louis, Missouri 63105 / 120 S. Central Ave., Suite 408	(314) 425-3134	William Duncan
Pac.	San Diego, California 92188 880 Front St., Suite 559	(619) 293-5360	Allan J. Rappoport
Pac.	San Francisco, California 94126 / 555 Battery St., P.O. Box 2450	(415) 556-4340	Paul Andrews
S.E.	San Juan, Puerto Rico 00903 P.O. Box 2112	(809) 723-2091	Paul E. Melendez
S.E.	Savannah, Georgia 31401 / 1 East Bay St.	(912) 944-4256	Gerald J. McManus
Pac.	Seattle, Washington 98174 909 First Ave.	(206) 442-0554	Robert Hardy
S.E.	Tampa, Florida 33602 301 S. Ashley Dr.	(813) 228-2381	Robert E. Perkins, Jr.
S.E.	Washington, D.C. 20041 / POB 17423 Gateway 1 Bldg., Dulles Intl. Apt., Chantilly, Va. 22021	(202) 566-8511	Sidney A. Reyes
S.E.	Wilmington, North Carolina 28401 One Virginia Ave.	(919) 343-4601	James Mahony

Telephone numbers listed are those which may be dialed commercially

Published by the United States Customs Service / Washington, D.C. 20229 (202) 566-3962 / **September 1985**

The "Lady Olga" appears to be a fishing boat to her very last inch of draft and beam and length. But she could be many other things; among them a well-disguised floating hideout. With her twin radars and a bouquet of net buoys, she would qualify as a working boat in any coast guard inspection. But at the same time, one could create a most comfortable working and living space aboard the Olga to accommodate any number of other activities.

A stern view of the Olga showing that you can easily hide a pebble among pebbles. Tied up with companion boats at a remote harbor, the crew enjoys that ultimate human right, complete freedom of action.

KAYSITE. Here's an easy way to obtain a floating home. First ask around your local boatyards for a vessel that is apparently beyond economic repair. There are a lot of them around so be selective. This old (67-years) fishing boat needed thousands of dollars worth of replanking and is typical of what you may find for little or nothing.

It's best to sandblast the hull but if you wire brush off all the loose crud the effect is almost the same. Then apply expanded wire mesh as shown.

Next, plaster on the special Kaysite mix (details from KAYSITE, 999 Old San Jose Rd., S 29, Soquel, CA 95073) and let the hull cure by keeping it moist for at least 10 days.

Then with a final coat of polyester resin, you're ready to go back in the water and live the free life!

Neat and attractive, this homemade houseboat provides its owner with much privacy despite a Sausalito marina location. It seems that people who live on the water intuitively understand the need to give their neighbors lots of space.

BIG old wooden boats are often available for little money since they require lots of maintenance. However, if you Kaysite one of these old tubs, your leakage problems will probably be over.

You are looking thru the door of a rather funky but comfortable houseboat towards the levee of Dutch Slough in the California Delta region. The "Sheila" is an old yacht which, like many others, travels from landing to landing. It can be thought of as a floating hideout since it is well-kept, fully licensed and the privacy seekers aboard never stage loud parties. At far right are two other small yachts that share the peace and tranquillity of this hideaway moorage. As an added bonus of this floating lifestyle is the fact that if you move around a lot you never have to pay rent. In summary, it is very possible that you will find this way of life habit-forming.

BUILD YOUR OWN FLOATING HIDEOUT

About ten years ago I was hiding out in the Delta and casting about for an interesting project. One day I found a set of large pontoons floating freely in the ship channel. I towed them back to my boat, cleaned and painted them. Then I was able to buy an old travel trailer for $75 and for another $25 put the two together to create a $100 houseboat. This is always a possibilty in an area where floating objects do break loose and wander around and old trailers are a bargain. But in case you don't have the same good luck, here's a super-simple houseboat that you can build from plans. Write Glen-L Marine Designs, 9152 Rosecrans, Bellflower, CA 90706 for more information on the boats shown on this and the following two pages.

CABIN PLANS

The **HUCK FINN CABIN PLANS** come in three sizes and are specifically designed for use with our "HUCK FINN" or "SUPER HUCK" PONTOONS. The construction methods used in these **CABIN PLANS** assures you of the lightest weight cabin consistent with strength and simplicity of building. The **8' CABIN** can be used on any version from 20' on up. The **12' CABIN** can be used on any model from 24' on up. And the spacious **16' CABIN** can be used on any model from 28' on up.

Whichever **CABIN PLAN** you select, you'll get a comfortable cabin arrangement which offers full headroom up to 6'-5" plus lots of light and ventilation. Each **CABIN PLAN** features a full 3' roof overhang at the front as well as a 4' "porch" both front and rear as a minimum. And on "SUPER HUCK" versions built to 10' beam, you have a 12" wide side deck each side also. Every arrangement has a control console and facilities for a galley as well.

The construction of the cabin is downright basic. The simple framework uses ordinary materials and fastenings to cut costs. The **CABIN PLANS** provide all the details for the windows, framing, and outside covering. Also provided are dimensions for all cabinets, settees, and partitions, PLUS printed procedural instructions complete with Bill of Materials.

While the arrangements shown are recommended, the manner in which you equip your **"HUCK FINN" CABIN** is up to your desires and requirements. However, remember that the "HUCK FINN" and "SUPER HUCK" PONTOONS are not ocean-going freighters. So keep materials and equipment as light in weight as possible. Note that the weight of the cabin structure, plus everything aboard, must NOT exceed the load capacity listed for the particular PONTOON version you are building. Be sure to check carefully the size **CABIN PLANS** you wish on the Order Form (see PRICE LIST).

NOTE: These CABIN PLANS do not include the plans and patterns required to build the basic "HUCK FINN" or "SUPER HUCK" pontoons and deck unit. These must be purchased separately. SEE PRICE LIST.

"HUCK FINN" CABIN CHARACTERISTICS

	8' Cabin	12' Cabin	16' Cabin
Cabin length	8'-0"	12'-0"	16'-0"
Cabin width	8'-0"	8'-0"	8'-0"
Roof length	12'-0"	16'-0"	20'-0"
Area on deck	64 sq. ft.	96 sq. ft.	128 sq. ft.
Height above deck	6'-6"	6'-6"	6'-6"
Sleeping capacity	2	4	6
Weight of structure (approx.)	500 lbs.	700 lbs.	900 lbs.

Construction: Lightweight plywood panel interior with 2" stud wall construction and cambered roof over three full length roof beams. Exterior covered with light gauge aluminum sheeting.

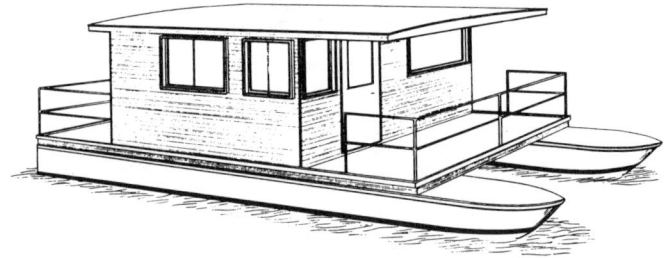

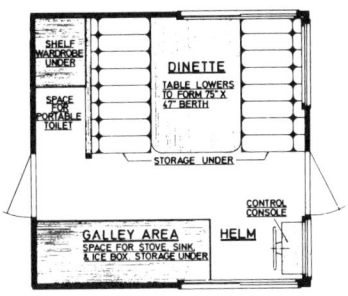

8' "HUCK FINN" CABIN PLANS

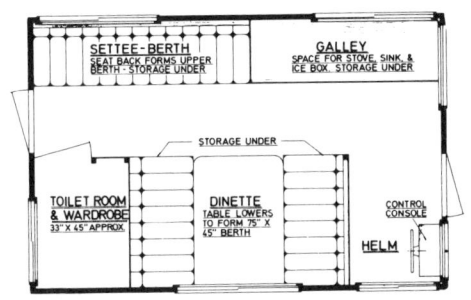

12' "HUCK FINN" CABIN PLANS

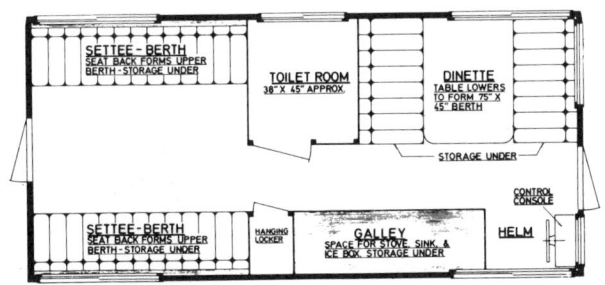

16' "HUCK FINN" CABIN PLANS

STARPATH 44 – CHARACTERISTICS

Length overall	43'-11"
Length waterline	35'-10"
Beam	14'-1½"
Draft (keel version)	6'-0"
Draft (C.B. version-board up)	4'-6"
Draft (C.B. version-board down)	9'-9"
Freeboard forward	6'-0"
Freeboard aft	5'-1"
Displacement	30,000 lbs.
Ballast weight	10,800 lbs.
Cabin headroom	6'-2" to 6'-7"
Fuel capacity	190 gals.
Fresh water capacity	200 gals.
Sleeping capacity	8
Sail areas - Sloop: Main	479 sq. ft.
Foretriangle	486 sq. ft.
Total	965 sq. ft.
Ketch: Main	372 sq. ft.
Foretriangle	446 sq. ft.
Mizzen	147 sq. ft.
Total	965 sq. ft.
Sail type:	Masthead rig in sloop or ketch configurations.
Power:	Single inboard gasoline or diesel engine of 30 to 50 shaft horsepower with suitable reduction gear.
Hull type:	Round bilge hull form with fixed ballast keel.

Building a floating hideout of this size can be a most worthwhile investment of your time and money. You can usually build for about 50% of the normal cost. Also, as soon as the hull is complete you can move into it as its caretaker. Most boat yards are very liberal in this area. Once afloat you have a home that can go anywhere on this planet with style and comfort. Try and beat that with an urban condo!

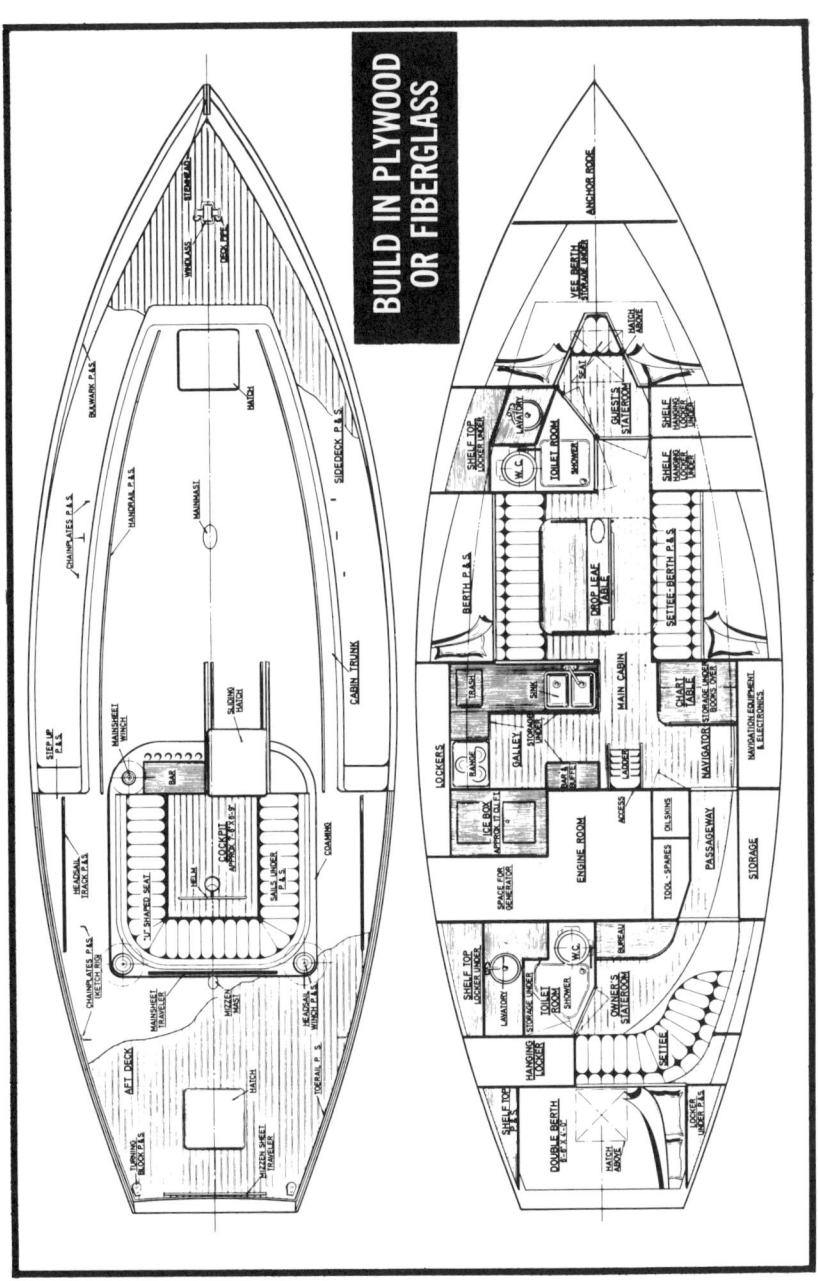

HOT SPRING HIDEOUTS

A chapter on hot springs as related to hideouts? Why not? A good hot spring can provide most every important creature need...warmth, water, cleansing, recreation, comfort, healing. If you've ever camped at a hot spring, you'll recall how wonderful it was to have an abundance of free, pure, hot or at least warm water. (Especially on a chilly night!) Because of this, selecting one of the 1700 plus hot springs in the eleven Western states as your hideout base could be a most wise decision.

WHERE TO FIND THEM

Hot springs are generously scattered among all Western states. Some areas have more than others (northern California, central Idaho) but no matter where you travel, you are probably not too far from a usable thermal spring. Fortunately, the majority are undeveloped and open for public use. A reference work on hot spring locations is *Great Hot Springs of the West* and may be found in most libraries. If not, write the author c/o the publisher for procurement information.

SOME TYPICAL SPRINGS

Ash Springs, NV. This is one of my favorite camping places and if you go there you'll see why. The springs run at a fantastic rate, a total of 5,000 gallons per minute from a group of sources. One in particular originates at the upper end of a small lake and is first contained in a small cemented pool shaded by willows and cottonwoods. It's open to the public all year at no charge, and as often as I've been there, I've found few people using it. With my trusty camper as a rolling hideout, I've spent many delightful days becoming as relaxed as a cooked noodle in the salubrious waters which are close to body temperature. All around are desert hills that provide challenging walks. Nights are filled with stars. Who could ask for more as a temporary refuge from this crazy planet?

Las Cruces Hot Spring, CA. This is a delightful twin pool offering temperatures from about 85 to 105. Only a half mile from Highway 101, it seems to be a million kilometers from anywhere because of its sylvan surroundings and totally natural environment. No charge, of course, and most users don't bother with bathing suits. If you are one of the mobile hideout people, you'll want to have an inventory of springs like this so you can wash the bod and the laundry without hassles.

Hot Creek, CA. What a great combination, a near-freezing trout stream and a hot springs that emerges as steam from the rocky creek bottom. The mixture produces an infinitely varied temperature from extra chilly to scalding. You have to monitor your location carefully but once you find the degree that matches your needs, aahhhh, it's so wonderful!

Not far from Highway 395 north of Bishop, this one should be on any tire tramp's list of top springs. Hard to reach through the snow in winter, it's still a delight any time you can make it.

Hot Lake, OR. This one is for those who like isolation, since it is about as remote as hot springs can be. Check the SE corner of Oregon for a strange sierra-like range of mountains called the Steens. Just east of them are a complex of springs of which Hot Lake is the largest. Once a source of borax, it is now open to the public anytime. Prepare yourself for an other-worldly experience since the lake is both large and deep, some say 7,000 feet. I recall the eerie experience of floating in water around 100 F and imagining more than a mile of hot water beneath me. Camping is no problem.

There's another smaller springs just a few miles SW of Hot Lake that doesn't appear on most maps. As you drive from the tiny village of Fields towards French Glen, keep your eyes open on the right for a plume of steam, especially on a cold day. A few tattered remnants of what might have been a development mark the spot. At least they were there the last time I was by, some years back.

Riverside Springs, ID. At least that's the name I've given them. You'll find them on both sides of the segment of Highway 93 (Pan American) that runs from Stanley to Clayton. Just keep your eyes open for steam. The water runs down into the Salmon river so, as with Hot Creek, you can select whatever temperature you like. This great spring is typical of the hundreds that you'll find in virtually-uninhabited Idaho. I highly recommend the state and its thermal wonders.

Spence Hot Springs, NM. While it gets plenty cold in this desert state, there are compensations and one of them is this great little springs located across the creek that parallels the access road. Free for public use, it's popular with the natives. So if you like company with your hot bath and some nearby camping spots, give this outdoor spa a try.

THERMAL SPRINGS AS SHORT OR LONG TERM HIDEOUTS

Moving around on wheels has to be one of the better things to do with one's life, at least that's my opinion after trying a lot of different ways to have fun. And having a warm outdoor bath waiting to cleanse and soothe your tired bod at the end of the day has to be one of the better ways to make traveling a constant delight.

As I envision it, one could invest in a tight little RV rig, develop some means of income on the road or from an outside source by some previous efforts, and then devote a few years to visiting every one of the accessible free hot springs in the western states.

I've been able to visit quite a few myself but I have many more to go. See you at one of the remote ones!

ABOVE: Rogers Hot Springs overlooking Lake Mead is open all year and there's no charge. Many remote canyons nearby.

TWO SOUTHERN NEVADA SPRINGS (In great hideout territory). ABOVE: Ash Springs is a fair-sized lake with a uniform temperature of about 85° F. BELOW: Another peaceful hideout hot springs available for a warm bath any time.

ABOVE: There's a pipe connecting the upper springs with the lower one at Las Cruces. Great for either laundry or a relaxing shower.

THE ULTIMATE HIDEOUT

It is not surprising that Jack London's novel of Big Brotherism, *The Iron Heel*, is seldom published or discussed in the U.S. After all, it calls the shots of the last seven or eight decades with uncanny accuracy. London's view of the future was undoubtedly a key factor in a more widely-known work, *1984* by George Orwell, since they have many similarities. Both books foresee huge populations controlled by shrewd, sinister and merciless oligarchs to whom power is the ultimate achievement, a goal transcending mere economic tyranny. One is reminded of the monolog by Richard III,

"Then, since this earth affords no joy to me, but to command, to check, to o'erbear such as are of better person than myself, I'll make my heaven to dream upon the crown."

The oppressed of *The Iron Heel* prefer death to a lack of liberty and thus wage a long-term battle with the tyrants. Part of their struggle involves concealment of their rebel cadre from the eyes and nooses of the sinister hunter/killer teams hired by the Iron Heelers. Thus, London conceives of an ultimate hideout which he describes as follows:

It was quite a scramble down to the stream bed and once on the bed we went down stream perhaps for a hundred feet. And then we came to a great hole. There was no warning of the existence of the hole nor was it a hole in the common sense of the word. One crawled through tight-locked briars and brambles and found oneself on the very edge peering out and down through a green screen. A couple of hundred feet in length and width, it was half of that in depth. Possibly because of some fault that had occurred when the knolls were flung together and certainly helped by freakish erosion, the hole had been scooped out in the course of centuries by the wash of water....

It was the perfect hiding place. No one ever came there, not even the village boys of Glen Ellen.

Jack goes on to describe how the guerillas live in the hideout for years without detection despite the fact that the mansion of a particularly rapacious oligarch is a short distance away.

There is much to be learned from London's story beyond his concept of the hideout that serves the rebels for nineteen years. It is not within the scope of this brief book to discuss it in detail so I strongly suggest you make every effort to find it in your library (rare) or in a used book store (possible).

From my own experience with hideouts and low-profile living, I am convinced that it CAN be done. Often difficult and demanding of one's patience, it is possible to not only create the ultimate hideout but to match it with the perseverance to accomplish whatever goals the hideout encompasses.

If the above were not true then every single spy would have been hanged and every VC would have been discovered in his underground tunnel. Obviously, this did not and could not occur.

Furthermore, from a pragmatic standpoint, the ultimate hideout is available in many areas. Oddly, about six months ago while taking a walk a few miles from my home, I wandered off the trail to investigate some odd shrubs. What a surprise to find a sink very similar to that described by London. Not as large but with all the other characteristics of remoteness, steep sides and very heavy vegetation shielding it from view. I envisioned someone building a highly secure and totally invisible hideout in the sheer wall of the sink close to or at the bottom. I cannot imagine anyone ever finding it as long as the person(s) using it were careful about their comings and goings.

How many Jack London/Iron Heel hideouts are there in the West? I would venture to guess there are tens of thousands and the majority available for use right now! Here are a few of the many places where you will find ultimate hideouts:

Southern Utah	Western Montana
Fort Huachuca, AZ	Southern Nevada
Northern New Mexico	Rocky Mountains, CO
High Sierras, CA	Northwest Wyoming
Central Idaho	Cascades, WA
Southeast Oregon	

Thus, in *all* Western states there are a variety of places where natural hideouts may be found, and we have really only mentioned a few. Go check them out for yourself. That's half the fun!

REPRISE

Let's see how London's super-hideout relates to the following parameters of hideout selection and design.

Security. This has to be the number one essential since without it you can forget all the other features. Jack's Glen

Ellen hideaway was secure because the power structure just could not imagine that the rebels they were seeking would be so audacious as to live almost on top of one of the Iron Heelers. The Sonoma valley, which is one of the locales in *The Iron Heel*, has many tangled arroyos and London chose the one that was really obvious, so obvious that no one ever thought of really looking at it!

Livability. No point of having a hideout if you can't really live there, and this element would include such factors as climate, water sanitation, pure air, possibility of growing your own food, availability of supplies, accessibility and cost (to own or lease). The latter implies that for some hideouts you would actually purchase the land or at least rent it. For others, the endless possibilities of squatting materializes which happens to be my personal preference. London's concept of a rebel stronghold had all of the above factors plus great natural beauty.

Enjoyment. Above and beyond mere livability is the essential of pure fun. It's my belief that if something isn't fun, it's just not worth doing. Too often have all of us been conned into doing all manner of unpleasant things for mere money, or status or alleged security. I say that enjoyment must be our first consideration for a hideout or anything else for that matter. On this score, Jack's hideout wins all the prizes.

SELF DEFENSE FOR YOUR HIDEOUT

The best defense is a gun. Handguns can be a hassle, since many states and localities have placed restrictions on their ownership. But rifles and shotguns are excellent defense weapons and can be legally purchased and owned just about anywhere.

> Henry David Thoreau once said:
>
> "I do not wish to kill or be killed, but I can foresee circumstances in which these things would be by me unavoidable. The question is not about weapons but the spirit in which you use them."
>
> Niccolo Machiavelli once commented:
>
> "Among other evils which being unarmed brings you, it causes you to be despised."
>
> George Washington, America's first president, said:
>
> "Firearms stand next to the Constitution in importance. The very atmosphere of firearms restrains evil interference — they deserve a place of honor with all that's good."

A good source of information on various available firearms is SHOTGUN NEWS, Hastings, NE. 68901. Send $2 for a sample copy. Tell them Wild Bill Kaysing sent you.

While they last!
The Original and most complete Receiver Kit! in STOCK!

STEN MKII
RECEIVER KITS

All Parts Necessary to Complete Armex, Sarco, or Other Sten MK II Internal Parts Kits ~~$80~~. **$69.50** ppd.

Our kit consists of:

- Special 1020 Steel receiver blank D.O.M. (Drawn over a mandrel to insure proper internal diameter and straightness.) Cut to correct length.
- An exclusive template pattern bonded to receiver blank showing the exact locations of all ports, slots, and holes - simply cut out marked areas with a small Dremel style tool or a hand drill and file.
- Barrel bushing already threaded for Bbl nut and is a 'slip fit' into our receiver.
- Hardened ejector easily fitted into receiver.
- Blueprint gives exact widths and dimensions of all ports, slots, and holes.
- Schematic to aid in assembly.
- Full step-by-step instructions.
- BATF Form-1 included for legal manufacture.

Build Your Own Selective Fire Sten Mk II In A Couple Of Hours With Simple Hand Tools, (no previous gunsmithing experience necessary).

We have hundreds of satisfied customers. Satisfaction Guaranteed or return unaltered kit within 2 weeks for full refund. NO FFL REQUIRED.

Get your MK II receiver kits while you still legally can! These are the best and most complete kits available

1 - $69.50 ea.
3 - $55.50 ea.
Call for quanitity discounts!

Send check, M.O. (C.O.D. add $3.50) to:
CATCO
316 California Ave., 341
Reno, NV 89509
or Call 707-253-8338

These sample ads from the pages of SHOTGUN NEWS show the wide variety of guns available.

STEN GUN MAGAZINES
Excellent Condition. **$2.00** each
Brand New **$3.00** each
New Parkerized **$3.00** each
Sten Mag. Loaders **$6.00** each
Hours: 12:00 Noon to 10:00 P.M.
7 Days A Week
TERMS: U.P.S. C.O.D., or Money orders in advance plus freight.

MANCHESTER ARMS
P.O. Box 129
Lenoir City, Tennessee 37771
JAMES McCOWN 1-615-986-2282

STEN GUN SPARE PARTS SETS - $89⁵⁰

EXTRA 32 RD MAGAZINES
$4.00 Ea. 10 For **$34.50**
25 For **$74.50**
100 For **$250.00**

NOTE: Check Your Local & ATF Regulations Before Assembling a Weapon From These Parts.

These are clearing customs now (late March) and should be in stock by the time this ad will be in print.

A complete set of spare parts for the STEN-MK II 9mm Submachinegun (except for the receiver). The "set" includes barrel, magazine, magazine housing, trigger housing and stock, a retainer, front threaded bushing, internal parts, bolt, etc. All parts except the receiver tube itself.
Parts are used - very good to excellent condition. As there is no receiver, no FFL is required.

Price - **$89.50** Kit
3 Kits for **$259.50**
10 Kits for **$750.00**

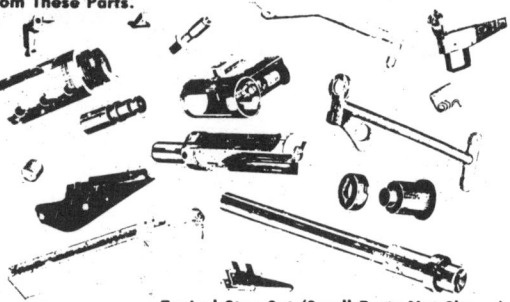

Typical Sten Set (Small Parts Not Shown)

MACHINE GUN
M-60

STILL THE BEST VALUE. NOW EVEN MORE AVAILABLE.

The M-60 Machine Gun, chambered in 7.62mm (NATO), is one of the most popular full-autos on the market. Because of the increasing interest in machine guns, Rock Island Armory is now concentrating on full-auto firearms, with special emphasis on the M-60. So now, high quality M-60's are in better supply than ever, and ready for 60-day delivery!

The Rock Island Armory M-60 is a carbon copy of the GI M-60 that first gained prominence in Viet Nam. Because it's so effective and so versatile, it's still the standard support weapon for U.S. combat ground troops. The Rock Island Armory M-60 is quality made, with a brand new, uncut and unwelded receiver. *And it's still the lowest priced, quality made M-60 on the market . . . one of the very best values anywhere!*

STILL JUST $1995

ORDERING INSTRUCTIONS
Include hand signed copy of current FFL with all orders. Cashiers check or money order must accompany all orders. Include sufficient funds for shipping/insurance. Illinois residents add 6% sales tax or include state sales tax number.

ROCK ISLAND ARMORY
Department D-7
420 West Main Street
Geneseo, Illinois 61254
(309) 944-2109

HIDEOUT CHOW

"As we grow more skillful in nomadic/wilderness living we find we can live well on less and less money. We eat what we forage plus bulk-purchased staples (wheat, brown rice, popcorn, soy, grits, lentils, powdered milk, vegetable oil, yeast, alfalfa seed which we sprout, vitamin C and E and honey)."

Innovator, March 1969

As I was winding up this book, it occurred to me that a word or two about the food one would eat in a hideout would be appropriate. This is especially true since living the free, outdoor life gives one a good appetite, one that should be satisfied with a better class of vittles. The best way to present my case is to quote from a book my wife Ruth and I wrote some years back titled, *Eat Well On a Dollar a Day*. Here, for your review, are excerpts.

A SUMMARY OF THE DOLLAR A DAY CONCEPT

Why It Is Important To Eat Better For Less

Most food sold in America is processed. That means it has had most of its food value removed and its remainder polluted with chemicals that are cumulatively harmful to humans. There is strong evidence that our one-in-four cancer rate is related to the increasing use of food additives.

Natural, Unprocessed Food Is Available Now

You don't have to wait another day to improve your health with a more natural diet. Go to your local natural food store and buy some basics. We've provided a starter list on another page. Other sources of good natural food include feed and grain stores, neighborhood co-ops (you can start your own), ranches and farms that use organic methods and foods you grow yourself. As the demand increases, more and more outlets exist.

You Can Make Delicious
Meals From Simple Ingredients

You'll never taste a better hot cereal than freshly ground whole grain wheat simmered slowly and then served with fresh fruit and a little milk or cream. This is just one example of hundreds of basic recipes available in numerous books. We provide a sampling herein. Freshly prepared food always tastes better than canned, frozen or otherwise processed meals. And it's not only less trouble than you think, it's fun!

Fresh, Raw Foods Are Best For Optimum Health

You can save time and energy costs by concentrating your diet around foods that are alive. Cooking kills the enzymes which are essential to assimilation. Therefore, if you eat plenty of fresh fruits and vegetables along with home-made sprouts, you'll regain and maintain your health.

Saving Money Is A Bonus

Ironically, the best food is the cheapest. Whole grain wheat is only $12 per hundred pounds by the sack. Conversely, cold cereals loaded with sugar and chemicals can cost up to $320 per hundred pounds!!!! (No wonder the cereal companies can spend millions on TV ads.)

THREE PROOFS

Proof Number One
The average person on this planet lives on food that costs less than 25¢ a day. They eat little meat, sugar and certainly nothing processed. Their health is better than most Americans.

Proof Number Two
Basic commodities are cheaper now than during the Great Depression. Wheat, oats, corn, and rice are at rock bottom when purchased in bulk form. You can buy a *year's supply* of these items for less than $100.

Proof Number Three
I practice what I preach and often eat well on much less than a dollar a day. I have more energy and strength than when I was half my present age (64).

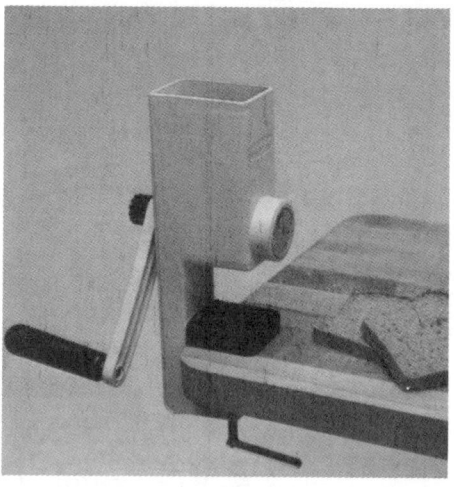

An ordinary kitchen blender will grind grain if you only put in about 4 ounces at one time. But if you can afford it, this type of home grinder would be one of the best hideout

equipment investments you could possibly make. It will grind grains, beans, seeds and just about anything in that broad category. Just imagine having freshly ground flour to make into hot biscuits and muffins. Nothing better!

PROOF POSITIVE

Here's a demonstration of the principle that we've presented on network TV many times (*Kathy Crosby Show, AM America, People are Talking, Ralph Storey Show* and dozens of others). It proves that you can eat well for a dollar a day or less, if you know how.

First acquire a quantity of whole grain wheat. Put four ounces in your kitchen blender and turn it to high (be sure the top is on tight, as those kernels would love to bounce all over your kitchen). Stick your fingers in your ears as this makes a lot of noise. Wait about 30 seconds and turn it off. You'll find that the blender has acted just like a small grain mill turning that hard wheat kernel into a combination of small and medium-sized particles. What you've produced is your own homemade Wheatena!

Boil a pint of water and pour in the fresh-ground grain and stir vigorously. Turn down the heat to the lowest setting and allow the cereal to simmer slowly with the lid on. In about 30 or 40 minutes, you'll have the best and freshest hot cereal you've ever tasted.

Add a little cream or milk, a few chopped nuts, a couple of cut up prunes, a tablespoon of raisins and some honey. Mmmmmm, you'll flip over the flavor! We guarantee it.

Your cost was just four cents for the cereal! This is on the basis that you bought the whole wheat in bulk form for about 12 to 15 cents per pound. Four ounces cooks up 12 ounces so you ended up with a big bowl of healthful food for a mere four pennies. Even if your additions ran 15 or 20 cents, you would still have enjoyed a big, hearty breakfast for under a quarter. And this example is why we are firmly convinced that anyone who wants to can have a better diet than they now have for *lots* less money. And the work involved is minimal and fun to boot!

HAD ANY BHA LATELY?

Try this test. Wander through the aisle of any supermarket and pick up various products from the shelves. Canned, bottled or packaged, you'll find that the majority contain dyes, bleaches, antioxidants, emulsifiers, preservatives, flavors, buffers, acidifiers, drying agents, sweeteners, anti-foaming agents, conditioners, hydrogenators and so forth ad infinitum. These take the form of such tasty chemical treats as calcium propionate, sodium benzoate, butylated hydroxianisole, nordihydroguaiaretic acid (NGDA) and Saforale.

Now, it wouldn't be so bad if we just had those to contend with. But what about the secondary reactions with the medications that so many people take? What happens when NGDA hits your Valium or BHA starts fighting with a Tums or Rolaid? To me, the wonder is not that half of America is sick; the wonder is that we're not all dead.

But stay with me dear reader; there's hope. You *can* avoid most of the dangerous chemicals if you bypass the processors. And that can be done by either growing more of your own food or getting it direct from a natural foods grower in bulk form. Try this test. Cut out anything that has a chemical additive for two weeks; see if your health doesn't improve markedly!

SOME STRATEGY

The American food industry is a $110 billion a year business. Somewhere between the farmer, who gets $30 billion, and the consumer, who pays the $110 billion, there is a large leak of $80 billion. In other words, the middlemen who promote and sell the food and control the prices we pay for it make a *gross* profit of $80 billion a year. It is the purpose of this book to encourage you to help reduce this leak or plug it up altogether by providing two kinds of information: how to eat what your body needs and wants (not what the industry says it should need and want); and how to avoid paying into the pockets of the middleman.

To eat well you must learn how to outwit some very clever minds. The food-industry moguls and their hired guns, the dirty rats on Madison Avenue, are very good at what they do. They managed to convince a huge proportion of the American people that we are getting our money's worth when we buy processed foods. They have accomplished this monumental feat (monumental considering the evidence to the contrary) in most cases by suppressing or simply ignoring the truth. To help you deal with these rascals, culprits, and con men, here are the basic rules:

(1) Plan on changing your entire way of life regarding food. No half-way measures will do if you really want to eat for less than a dollar a day.

(2) Develop a sense of humor as well as a sense of strategy. Think of yourself as a guerilla in a funny/serious war with rats who are trying to profit from your presumed gullibility. But keep in mind that the last laugh will be yours, since you are fully capable of using your head in finding out the truth on your own.

(3) Stay out of supermarkets except when shopping for fresh foods and possibly dairy products.

(4) Search out and buy from alternative food sources.

(5) Plan on keeping lots of bulk foods in your home at all times. That way you will reduce your shopping trips and will be protected in case of disaster.

(6) Be open-minded. Try new foods, both wild and domestic.

(7) Plant a garden; the bigger it is the better for your pocketbook. There are good books on the subject in your local library and book store, and more are coming out all the time.

(8) Learn about harvest times for local crops. Take a weekend drive in the country and make it a food-gathering trip.

(9) Think of meat as a condiment, not as a staple.

(10) Give up sugar and all sugar-containing products. It's easier to do than you may think, and the reasons for doing it are pressing, as you will learn.

(11) Buy international cookbooks. Find out what people in other cultures eat and try their recipes.

(12) Eat raw foods or let things cook themselves. Save time and energy (yours and the kind you pay for).

(13) Eat less. Determine your own minimum requirements and keep to them.

(14) Don't waste anything.

(15) Make your own convenience foods. You can even make money doing this if you're creative and enterprising enough.

> You can read more about the situation in such books as:
>
> FOOD FOR PEOPLE NOT FOR PROFIT, Lerza and Jacobson
>
> COMMERCIAL FOODS EXPOSED, G. Horsley
>
> THE CHEMICAL FEAST, James Turner
>
> THE POISONS IN YOUR FOOD, William Longgood
>
> EAT YOUR HEART OUT: PROFITEERING IN AMERICA, Jim Hightower
>
> CONSUMER BEWARE, B.T. Hunter

BULK FOODS

Here's a sampling of basic bulk foods that will provide you with a good inventory for your pantry. To start out, buy a pound or two of each to see how you like them. Add and subtract items to suit your own palate and budget. We have found that with these items in our kitchen, we only need add perishables like fruits, vegetables, eggs and so forth to be able to rustle up some great meals.

Whole Wheat: This is the anchor of our diet. By sprouting it, we have a fresh vegetable. By cooking it whole, we have a bean substitute, and by grinding it, we can enjoy fresh cereal, breads, biscuits, and a wide variety of delicious desserts. As of this writing, the bulk price of wheat has gone down due to bumper crops. Even if it goes up slightly, it's still a bargain.

Whole Corn: We love this stuff! It's useful in so many ways that we couldn't be without it. One of the best methods is to grind it in your blender, boil it up, and use it as a breakfast cereal, or chilled with added fruits or meats as scrapple. Corn slumped in price too last year.

Alfalfa Seed: Why do we list this third? Simply because sprouted seeds can provide you with almost all the vitamins you need. Not only that, you can sprout them anytime, under almost any circumstances.

Mung Beans: Get these for the same reason: they make delicious, giant-sized sprouts even in the dead of winter.

Soy Sauce: A seasoning that's vital to the success of your Chinese dishes. Buy it in a Chinese market if possible to get the real thing at low cost.

Sea Salt: An important staple; a little goes a long way. If it's from the sea, you get the trace minerals free.

Honey: The best sweetener you can buy, and it contains more food value than any other natural sugar.

Assorted Spices: A mixture of cumin, paprika, pepper, curry powder, and others. (We like to grow our herbs at home, or gather them wild.)

Non-Instant Powdered Milk: Surprise! We do use this for cooking and drinking, but we use it even more for making yogurt. With the nutritional changes that take place during this process, you gain tremendously on your investment. Powdered buttermilk is a delightful variation that's great for making pancakes and other recipes where dry milk is specified.

Brewer's Yeast: One of the best natural sources of vitamins and minerals. Brewer's yeast can be added to drinks, pancake batter, or just eaten plain by the spoonful, if you can stand the taste!

Brown Rice: Rice is a universal food, useful in dozens of ways. Just be sure that it's brown and not white, since the latter has no real food value beyond carbohydrates.

Soybeans: Another great staple, loaded with protein, vitamins, and iron.

Pinto Beans: We saw these on special for just 20 cents a pound because they were split. This is no disadvantage; in fact, they'll cook faster this way. With beans and corn in the cupboard, no Mexican feels deprived. One can make countless tasty dishes from this combination. Actually, you might pay even less if you bought 50 or 100 pounds.

Potatoes: One of the most useful foods in anyone's larder, and delicious too. The Irish lived on a potato diet for many decades and worked up enough energy to migrate to the U.S.!

Onions: If you buy them at the right time of year and store them carefully, they'll last a long time. Added to any diet, onions spell good flavor and nutritional value. In fact, they're the basic flavoring for most peasant dishes.

Assorted Nuts: A useful source of protein. Nuts can be used in main dishes or for healthful snacks anytime.

Safflower Oil: We use this for cooking, frying, and salad dressings. Stay with the cold-pressed oils — safflower, soy, olive, and sesame are good ones. Use them sparingly, since they're expensive.

Raisins: Raisins are expensive but provide good food value. A few added to many a recipe adds flavor and interest.

Dates: If you buy the dry variety, they are often relatively cheap.

A MISCELLANY

Here are some miscellaneous ideas that will help you create a great hideout for yourself anywhere in the West.

COMPUTERS AND HIDEOUTS

By now, most of us are quite familiar with the availability and application of home computers. Inexpensive (and getting more so), quite reliable, and useful in many ways to those out of the mainstream, a home computer can make the difference between a so-so hideout and one that yields many dividends.

For instance, you can operate a home business with a computer keeping track of ads, response rates, orders, back-orders, and so forth. You would be able to write quickly and revise promptly using one of the word processor software programs. With a modem (a telephone link) you can connect to many sources of valuable data. Want information on traveling? Then join CompuServe or The Source. Either one will send you tons of data on the history, current status and main attractions of almost any locale. They will also alert you to places that might be dangerous due to social instability or health problems. Their addresses are: CompuServe, 5000 Arlington Centre Blvd., Columbus, OH 43220; and The Source, 1616 Anderson Rd., McLean, VA 22101.

Your local library is awash with books on home computer use so we won't waste space on redundancy. For the hardware, a good source is Radio Shack. Software is available in abundance and some sources are:

Electronic Magazines such as *Byte*; and *The Whole Earth Software Catalog*, $15 PP from *Whole Earth*, 27 Gate Five Rd., Sausalito, CA 94965

ELECTRONIC SECURITY FOR YOUR HIDEOUT

No one need surprise you in your hideout, considering the great abundance of devices now on the market. For example, the black box below is capable of selectively identifying sounds made by breaking glass, pry bars and wood and so forth. It ignores the ordinary sounds of daily life, but should someone try to break in, it blows whistles, activates sirens, turns on lights or does whatever you wish it to do. The information on short wave may be of value if you want to set up your own communications links. On the next three pages is a fantastic inventory of plans and kits for devices that should put you slightly ahead of that IRS special agent who has been trying to creep up on you.

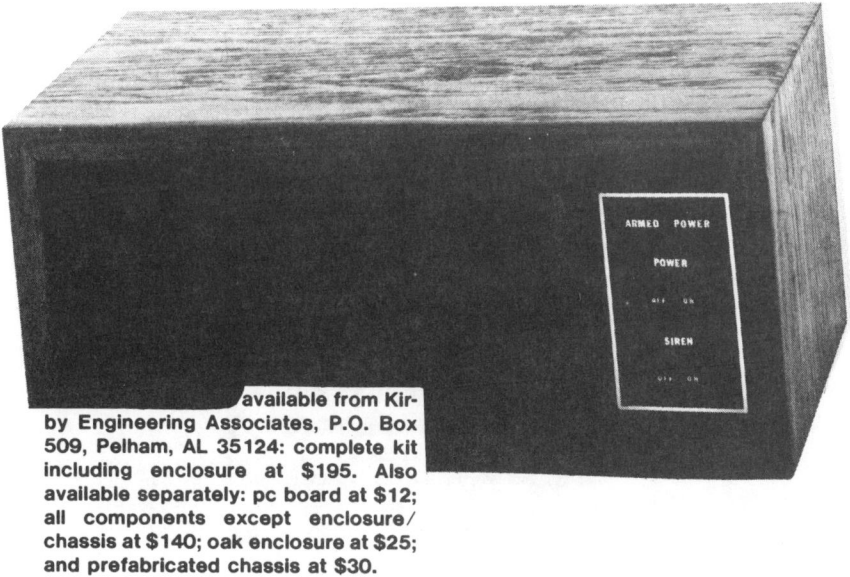

available from Kirby Engineering Associates, P.O. Box 509, Pelham, AL 35124: complete kit including enclosure at $195. Also available separately: pc board at $12; all components except enclosure/chassis at $140; oak enclosure at $25; and prefabricated chassis at $30.

The DOUBLE FARFOON™ Distant Sound Detector

1984 brings this brand new sound-gathering instrument. It has twice the power of other types. Four band pass filters let you TUNE OUT the frequencies you do not want which might interfere with the sounds you are seeking. Dial what you want. Dial out what you don't want. Two channels amplify all sound frequencies. This versatile instrument comes with a standard 3½ inch parabolic nose cone sound collector. Interchangeable larger collectors come as optional equipment for special requirements. You get much greater directional sound gathering with these parabolic collector assemblies. Send for free literature today about the DOUBLE FARFOON and The "Super Ear", another sound detecting unit we offer at under $100 for various detection purposes.

Don't Buy Any Distant Sound detectors Until you get our prices. We have a COMPLETE range of instruments from the BIONIC EAR to Super Ear. Hunters Ear and the Double Farfoon (illustrated). Lowest prices.
WRITE TODAY
FREEMAN ELECTRIC CO.
1010 Cook Bldg., Freeman, MO 64746
(816) 221-8840

How to Tune the Secret Shortwave Spectrum
by Harry L. Helms

Clandestine broadcasters are stations whose programs are intended for reception by a certain region or segment of the world's population. They are distinguished from ordinary broadcasters by any or all of three factors: they are extralegal in some respects; they are political creations; and there is some element of deception in their operation. In one of the most interesting books on DXing I have run across, Harry Helms describes the range of clandestine radio stations—from those operated by anti-communist guerrillas in Southeast Asia, to Soviet manned-spaceflight communications, to high school r-f bootleggers in Minnesota. And there's more: Basques who seem to be transmitting from northern Spain, but whose transmitter is actually in Venezuela; strange coded messages originating in South Dakota, whose purpose is unknown but presumed to have something to do with the Minuteman missile fields; spy rings in Croatia; you-name-it. If you want to check some of this stuff out on your own set, the author gives lots of frequencies and times to choose from, plus suggestions about the equipment you'll need.

Published by *TAB Books, Inc.*, Blue Ridge Summit, PA 17214. Soft Cover. 182 pages. $6.95

PRIVACY·SECURITY·SAFETY·SURVIVAL

BOMB SPY CCX 1000
The Bomb Spy CCX 1000 electronically "sniffs out" explosive vapors and protects against false alarms with a built-in verification system. The CCX 1000 is small and lightweight yet supersensitive. A continuous series of audible beeps warns of a true explosive. The CCX 1000 can effectively scan people, packages or luggage in just seconds.

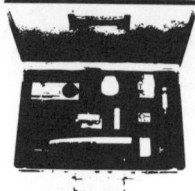

SURVEILLANCE SYSTEMS

PORTABLE WIRELESS TELEPHONE SC 225 P
The SC 225 P provides super long range wireless communications in a portable system. With its convenient shoulder strap and lightweight rugged exterior, the SC 225 P can easily travel into a surveillance situation or anywhere telephones are not available. The SC 225 P can provide crystal clear conversation up to an incredible 2500 kilometer range from its base station.

MINIATURE VOICE STRESS ANALYZER™
Used for years by professionals, the VSA has now been ultra miniaturized. The new Mini VSA is portable and compact so that it can be carried in a briefcase, used in offices and many other discrete situations. This is still the same high quality system that analyzes a person's voice to detect stress and deception. It alerts you to lies with a simple digital readout. The Mini VSA can analyze even tape recorded telephone conversations.

WALKIE TALKIE SCRAMBLER X 222
The X 222 protects a walkie talkie conversation from eavesdroppers. Crowded airwaves provide little if any privacy. With the flip of a switch, the X 222 gives you the security of speaking with a privacy scrambler.

NIGHTFINDER TH 70
See through dense smoke, fog or total darkness. The TH 70 is a hands-free system that allows you to continue driving, flying or working without light. The lightweight goggles strap around your head to leave the hands free. With its passive light intensification source, the TH 70 needs no more light than a single star.

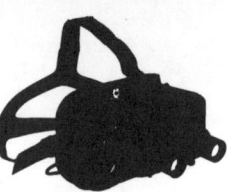

INVISIBLE SURVEILLANCE SYSTEM JVR 500
The JVR 500 flashes an invisible beam that can be seen only with a special infrared viewer. The JVR can be discreetly hidden in cargo, luggage, vehicles or clothing. The flashing beam lets you keep track of valuable items or locate items in a crowd. Because the infrared viewer is so compact, it can be used in discrete surveillance or undercover work.

SURVEILLANCE KIT
(For Law Enforcement Only)
This specialized kit contains 35 types of miniature long range transmitters, laser and optical transmitters for room audio and telephones. Any U.S. inquiries must be submitted on official letterhead by authorized personnel only.

 CCS COMMUNICATION CONTROL INC.

WORLD HEADQUARTERS
633 Third Ave., New York, N.Y. 10017
212-697-8140 TX: 238720

USA OFFICES
1801 K St. N.W., Washington D.C. 20006
202-659-3432
1435 Brickell Ave., Miami, Fla. 33131 305-358-4336
320 N. Michigan Ave., Chicago, Ill. 60601
312-726-0998
The Galleria, Suite 3405, Houston, TX. 77056
713-626-0007
9465 Wilshire Blvd., Beverly Hills, Ca. 90212
213-274-6256

EUROPEAN OFFICES
26 Place Vendome/35 Rue Danielle Casanova,
75001 Paris France 4-297-5600 TX: CCS215524F
62 S. Audley St., London W1 England
01-629-0223 TX: 8814709
COPYRIGHT CCS 1984

COUNTER SURVEILLANCE

Suspect someone's watching you? Have terminal paranoia? Then it might be worthwhile to look into the products of SECURETRONICS, PO Box 18696, Tucson, AZ 85731. As they say, "in today's world it takes more than a toy to insure your privacy."

CATALOG OFFER

For just $1 you can obtain a most interesting catalog from EMF, 1900 E. Warner St. 1D, Santa Ana, CA 92705. If you don't find it suitable to a hideaway lifestyle, I will refund your $1.

SILENT PROTECTION

When crossbows were invented, the age of armor was over since crossbow bolts went through armor like a hot knife through butter. Today, high tech has ensured that this type of weapon is even more efficient while still retaining the all-important advantage of complete silence of operation.

Incidentally, crossbows have been the favorite tool of poachers on the King's domain. Thus, if you can't afford a hunting license, this may be the way to go.

NEW YORK DIVISION
7 CENTRE MARKET PL. DEPT. SN
NEW YORK, N.Y. 10013
ORDER DESK 1-800-221-9408
INFO. (212) 925-4111/2

CONN. DIVISION
P.O. BOX 385 DEPT. SN
998 N. COLONY RD.
MERIDEN, CT 06450
ORDER DESK 1-800-243-3404
INFO. (203) 238-4285/6

69% SUCCESS ON ELK
79% SUCCESS ON DEER

"River of No Return" wilderness area. Our block of 256,000 acres in the center of wilderness produces consistent success. Elk, Mulies, Bear and Cougar. Great food, super accommodations. Fly-in or boat-in only. No roads within 15 miles.

Call or write for information.

SHEPP RANCH IDAHO
Dept. SN, P.O. Box 8013
Redwood City, CA 94063
(415) 367-0200

CROSSBOWS
Commando, 175 lb. $286.95
Panzer, 150 lb. $125.00
Wildcat I, 150 lb. .... $ 99.00
Wildcat II, 150 lb. $134.95
Thunderbolt, 125 lb. (Compound.) ... $249.95
Trident, 45 lb. (Pistol). .... $ 64.95
IMP, 30 lb. (Pistol). .... $ 39.95
Thunderbolt (Paratrooper).......... $184.95

BOLTS
Trident w/field point (5). .... $ 9.50
IMP - 14-P Bolts, (10). .... $ 7.15
Alum. Bolt w/field Pt. (5). .... $ 14.35
Alum. Bolt w/broadhead (5). .... $ 15.95
Fiberglass Bolt w/field pt. (5)....... $ 14.35

ACCESSORIES
Footclaw for Crossbow. .... $ 19.95
Footclaw for Trident. .... $ 19.95
Trident revolving bbl. w/3 bolts..... $ 22.75
Trident, 75 lb. prod. .... $ 22.75
String for Trident on IMP. .... $ 3.15
String for Crossbow. .... $ 3.45

SPEAKING OF LAND

Here are some selections from a recent issue of *Shotgun News* that sound like appropriate selections for hideout seekers.

$50. DOWN 5-40 acres. Washington, Idaho, Montana. from $5950.; Homesteading, Retirement, Recreation; Northwest Timberlands, Dept. SH 1323 North Ash, Spokane, WA 99201. **7-3XX**

FREE 20 ACRE Mountain retreats available. Real property. Income tax advantages. Details, SASE; WMMCO, Box 118, Lake George, CO 80827. **7-3X**

IDAHO LAND FOR SALE. For the outdoor person, good hunting & fishing, gentle year around weather. Four to twenty acres on or viewing The Clear Water River. Ideal for recreation, retirement, hills, woods & view. Twenty miles from the Selway Bitterroot Wilderness. Financing available; Empire Realty, Karen Smith, Box 951, Kamiah, ID 83536. 1-208-935-0468. **12-3X**

POPULATION DENSITY

That's an important concern for hideout seekers. For instance, New Jersey has 1006 residents per square mile, while Massachusetts has 714. Compare that to the table below:

STATE	PEOPLE PER SQUARE MILE
California	164
Oregon	28
Washington	65
Idaho	12
Montana	6
Wyoming	5
Utah	20
Colorado	31
New Mexico	12
Arizona	27
Nevada	8
Alaska	1

EQUIPMENT FOR YOUR HIDEAWAY

Infra-red sensors, low-cost transformers, 12-volt water pumps — these and many other useful items can be obtained from the Surplus Center, 1015 West "O" St., PO Box 82209, Lincoln, NE 68501. Their catalog is free.

A FUN WAY TO FIND A HIDEOUT LOCATION

Just invest in a rubber raft, the usual camping gear and a book on high adventure and great courage. Then you'll be ready to float down any river in the west and explore all the tributaries. For starters, I suggest the wonderful River of No Return, the Salmon in colorful Idaho.

SUMMARY AND CONCLUSIONS

As you have seen in words and pictures, there *are* hideouts in the Great American West at the present time and many people enjoy this free lifestyle. We have presented *ideas* about the hideout concept so that you can use your own creative imagination to develop a hideout that will be all that you desire.

I believe that we have shown that hideouts are, above all, fun — an exciting escape from the humdrum existence that the Corporate State programs as an imperative. Also, hideouts can be inexpensive as well as healthful. A funky log cabin in the woods amidst fresh air and pure water could restore almost anyone's budget and well-being.

Two major conclusions can be drawn:

(1) With increasing encroachment on the individual's private life, a hideout makes good sense.

(2) Considering how much open land and water is available, one has an extensive inventory of choices.

Try a great hideout in the West. I think you'll enjoy the experience and broaden your physical and spiritual horizons.

BIBLIOGRAPHY

Here is a sampling of books useful to the hideout creator.

DESIGN FOR A LIMITED PLANET, Skurka & Naar, Ballantine Books, 201 E. 50th St., New York, NY 10022. Excellent source book for alternative housing showing use of adobe, glass bottle, beer cans and other natural or recycled materials. Appropriate for hideout builders on a low budget.

WIN YOUR PERSONAL TAX REVOLT, Bill Greene, Harbor Publishing Co., 1668 Lombard St., San Francisco, CA 94123. One of the best books on both legal and hanky-panky tax avoidance by a genius who was so dangerous to the IRS they put him away for a while. He's now in a hideout of his own selection.

HOW TO EARN A LIVING IN THE COUNTRY, Wm. Osgood, Garden Way Pub., Charlotte, VT 05445. Pragmatic review of what can be done to acquire an income if you live outasite. Has extensive bibliography and the publisher has many other books of a similar nature.

BACKYARD BONANZA, Rodale Press, Emmaus, PA 18099. Only a pamphlet, but replete with tips on how to grow the most food in the smallest space. All you really need to be food independent in the boondocks. Publisher has many similar publications. Send for their catalog if this is one of your directions.

OUTLAWS OF THE OCEAN, Mueller and Adler, Hearst Marine Books, 105 Madison Av., New York, NY 10016. If you spend time at sea on a floating hideout you should know what the new hazards are and this book is up to date on the subject.

THE AGE OF SURVEILLANCE, F.J. Donner, Knopf, same address as Ballantine, given above. A monumental work, exhaustively researched, providing the history and current status of how Big Brother keeps his eye on you. And if you know how, then you can plan avoidance measures.

A NEW BREED OF DOCTOR, Alan H. Nittler MD, Pyramid Books, 919 Third Av., New York, NY 10022. One of the best books ever written on staying healthy through good nutrition. Millions were sold in paperback so a used bookstore might be the best source. Remember, hideouts aren't much fun unless you feel top notch and food is basic to well-being.

ATTIC CONVERSION, (video tape), R. Roskind, Owner Builder Center, 1515 Fifth St., Berkeley, CA 94710. (About $20.) One of a series of video cassettes on how to master basic carpentry, plumbing, wiring, interiors, etc. Could be more helpful than a book if you are an amateur at hideout building. Incidentally, send for a list of books from this group. They have some fine ones.

OFF THE BEATEN PATH, Harian Publications, 1 Vernon Av., Floral Park, NY 11001. One of several books on relatively undiscovered hideaways in the U.S. Send for their catalog.

THE SIERRA CLUB GUIDE TO THE NATURAL AREAS OF OREGON AND WASHINGTON, John and Jane Perry, Sierra Club Books, 201 E. 50th St., New York,

NY 10022. One of several well-researched books on the uncrowded parts of the West. As the authors point out, 95 percent of all travelers crowd into five percent of the available wildlands. This book discusses some of the other 95 percent. For a catalog of Sierra Club Books write them at 2034 Fillmore St., San Francisco, CA 94115.

MICROS, MINIS AND MAINFRAMES, Werner and Warner, Chilton Book Co., Radnor, PA 19089. While there are hundreds of new books on computing published every year, this one is outstanding because it provides additional sources of help at the end of each chapter. For example, if you propose to use your hideout as a writing studio, you'll learn about word processing in a few pages and then be invited to pursue the subject in many other books and periodicals. Also offers an extensive inventory of both hard and software sources and descriptions.

SHELTERS, SHACKS AND SHANTIES, D.C. Beard, Loompanics Unlimited, PO Box 1197, Port Townsend, WA 98368. Positively the best book on building hideouts ever published. First printed in 1914, it now appears in a paperback complete with great detailed drawings of treehouses, bog kens (houses built in marshes on stilts) and "all-American boy" underground houses. You won't need any other guide book on hideout shelter, I guarantee it.

START-UP MONEY, Mike McKeever, Nolo Press, PO Box 544, Occidental, CA 95465. This valuable guide for the hideout entrepreneur who wants money to start up a mail-order business is typical of the offerings of Nolo. They also offer a number of legal guides allowing anyone to avoid lawyers, a most worthy objective I'm sure you'll agree.

SURVIVAL INTO THE 21st CENTURY, V. Kulvinskas, Omangod Press, PO Box 225, Wethersfield, CT 06109. You may find this great compendium of information in a used book store and I suggest you look. From its introduction by Dick Gregory to the extensive bibliography, it is loaded with data that can help you regain your health and then keep it.

HOMEMAKING AROUND THE WORLD, Dept of State, AID, Washington, DC 20523. Another used bookstore item, this one tells how to make a stove from clay and a fridge that doesn't need ice. I liked the description of a Nigerian kitchen with a stove made from kerosene tins, cups and mixing bowls from gourds, a grinder from stones. With this book you can furnish your hideout using castoff items and natural materials.

BACK TO EDEN, Jethro Kloss, Longview Publishers, Coalmont, TN 37313. Lots of these around since it is one of the best-selling books on natural diet and health. Good old Jethro tells about the Chinese who buy our sage and drink it as tea while they sell us *their* tea which can cause great distress. Pointers on the use of herbs, homemade remedies and some wonderful recipes; all in all, a fine reference book for any successful hideout. Try used book stores.

THE AQUARIAN CONSPIRACY, Marilyn Ferguson, J.P. Tarcher, 9110 Sunset Bl., Los Angeles, CA 90069. Subtitled "PERSONAL AND SOCIAL TRANSFORMATION IN THE 1980's," this is my own personal selection for a hideout library must. Gives support to your often-felt and yet seldom-expressed inner view. I read this once a year and gain strength from its timeless wisdom.

WORDS FROM THE SOURCE, Louis Gittner, Prentic Hall, Englewood Cliffs, NJ 07631. Book can be ordered from Louis Foundation PO Box 210, Eastsound, WA 98245. Louis is a good friend and provides the straight skinny about our connections with the cosmos. When you are out there in the boondocks, it might be advisable to plug into some cosmic energy and this book tells how it can be done.

FAREWELL AMERICA, James Hepburn, Frontiers Pub. Co., Vaduz, Liechtenstein. Hard to find, but worth the effort, this book was printed in Europe because it was just too hot for America. A rational, well-documented description of how and *why* JFK was assassinated. Important information for anyone who wants to know just how the real government operates.

PLANNING FOR WELLNESS, Ardell and Tager, Kendall Hunt Pub. Co., 2460 Kerper Bl., Dubuque, IA 52001. I've read a lot of books on health but this one goes far beyond the usual "eat vegies and exercise." It reflects the Zen concept of "to *do* is to *be* and vice versa" and emphasizes lifestyle as the paramount consideration. A must for any far-roaming searcher for the truth in all things.

WHOLE EARTH REVIEW, 27 Gate Five Rd., Sausalito, CA 94965. Not a book, but a fine periodical (4 issues $18). It presents tools and ideas for the computer age. An entertaining way to keep up with what's new in hideout technology, etc.

YOU WILL ALSO WANT TO READ:

☐ **UNINHABITED AND DESERTED ISLANDS,** *by Jon Fisher.* This unique book covers more than 150 uninhabited and deserted islands in the remote regions of the world, from the Pacific Ocean to the Antarctic, from the Atlantic to the Indian Ocean. Each island is described as to history and physical conditions, and maps are included to show the exact location of each uninhabited island. *5½ x 8½, 116 pp, over 40 maps, indexed, soft cover. $7.95.* (Order Number 17024).

☐ **HOW TO BUY LAND CHEAP,** *by Edward Preston.* This practical book covers where to start, buying land for back taxes, buying land at private auctions, inside tips, and other ways to buy land cheap. Also includes a glossary of terms, information sources, diagrams and explanations of land descriptions, and more. Highly recommended for survivalists, retreaters, drop-outs, homesteaders, and anyone else interested in buying land cheap. *5½ x 8½, 3rd Edition, 94 pp, illustrated, soft cover. $6.95.* (Order Number 14046).

☐ **THE LAST FRONTIERS ON EARTH: Strange Places Where You Can Live Free,** *by Jon Fisher.* This exciting and amazing book discusses living in Antarctica, on floating icebergs, on floating ocean platforms, in underwater habitats, living as a nomad, living in an airship, and much more. Each idea is discussed in detail as to what it would cost, the availability of food and shelter, climate and other pertinent factors. Freedom of choice always exists for those who seek it — this is a book for freedom seekers. *5½ x 8½, 144 pp, illustrated, soft cover. $8.95.* (Order Number 17032).

LOOMPANICS UNLIMITED/PO BOX 1197/PORT TOWNSEND, WA 98368

Please send me the books I have checked above. I am enclosing $ ....
(which includes $3.00 for shipping and handling).
Name ....
Address ....
City/State/Zip ....

We offer the very finest in controversial and unusual books. Please see the catalog announcement on the next page.   **GHW**

"Yes, there are books about the skills of apocalypse -- spying, surveillance, fraud, wire-tapping, smuggling, self-defense, lockpicking, gunmanship, eavesdropping, car chasing, civil warfare, surviving jail, and dropping out of sight. Apparently writing books is the way mercenaries bring in spare cash between wars. The books are useful, and it's good the information is freely available (and they definitely inspire interesting dreams), but their advice should be taken with a salt shaker or two and all your wits. A few of these volumes are truly scary. Loompanics is the best of the Libertarian suppliers who carry them. Though full of 'you'll-wish-you'd-read-these-when-it's-too-late' rhetoric, their catalog is genuinely informative."
-THE NEXT WHOLE EARTH CATALOG

Now available:
THE BEST BOOK CATALOG IN THE WORLD!!!

- Large 8½ x 11 size!
- More than 500 of the most controversial and unusual books ever printed!!!
- YOU can order EVERY book listed!!!
- Periodic Supplements to keep you posted on the LATEST titles available!!!

We offer hard-to-find books on the world's most unusual subjects. Here are a few of the topics covered IN DEPTH in our exciting new catalog:

- Hiding/concealment of physical objects! A complete section of the best books ever written on hiding things!
- Fake ID/Alternate Identities! The most comprehensive selection of books on this little-known subject ever offered for sale! You have to see it to believe it!
- Investigative/Undercover methods and techniques! Professional secrets known only to a few, now revealed for YOU to use! Actual police manuals on shadowing and surveillance!
- And much, much more, including Locks and Locksmithing, Self Defense, Intelligence Increase, Life Extension, Money-Making Opportunities, and much, much more!

Our book catalog is truly THE BEST BOOK CATALOG IN THE WORLD! Order yours today -- you will be very pleased, we know.

(Our catalog is free with the order of any book on the previous page -- or is $2.00 if ordered by itself.)

Loompanics Unlimited
PO Box 1197
Pt Townsend, WA 98368
USA